I0763065

MARSHFIELD, THE RESIDENCE OF MR. WEBSTER.

MR. WEBSTER AT MARSHFIELD.

PROFILE SKETCH OF MR. WEBSTER.

MR. WEBSTER'S BIRTH-PLACE.

THE PRIVATE LIFE

OF

DANIEL WEBSTER.

BY CHARLES LANMAN.

He that hath the vantage-ground to DO GOOD, is an HONEST MAN.—*Bacon.*

NEW YORK:
HARPER & BROTHERS, PUBLISHERS,
329 & 331 PEARL STREET,
FRANKLIN SQUARE.
1852.

PRELIMINARY NOTE.

The writer of this little volume was attached to its distinguished subject by the official tie of private secretary, and also by the endearing ties of admiration for a great intellect, and the strongest attachment to a most noble Heart and the best of Friends. He has frequently visited *Elms Farm* in New Hampshire, and *Marshfield* in Massachusetts, as the friend and guest of their distinguished proprietor; and while in their vicinity, it was natural that he should have had opportunities of gathering from the older inhabitants, and other authentic sources, many incidents of personal history. These were, for the most part, repeated to him for his own gratification; but, now "that the mold," in the statesman's own words, "is beginning to gather upon the tomb" of Daniel Webster, the writer has deemed it his duty to present them to the public for their edification and pleasure. His fame as a patriot, a jurist, a statesman, an orator, and a scholar, is coextensive with the civilized world, and it can not but be of essential service to the rising generation, and agreeable to all admirers of intellectual greatness, to become acquainted with some of the facts which tend to illustrate the every-day life and personal character of such a man. In the following pages a regular biography has by no means been attempted; it was only the writer's intention to narrate, in a simple and unpretending manner, a collection of authentic personal memorials, which may tend to embellish the extensive biographies of Webster which will hereafter be added to our national literature.

CHARLES LANMAN.

Washington, November, 1852.

CONTENTS.

Page
BIRTH AND BOYHOOD 9
COLLEGE DAYS 23
EARLY LEGAL CAREER 35
ELMS FARM 48
MARSHFIELD 69
TRAITS OF PERSONAL CHARACTER 83
MISCELLANEOUS MEMORIALS 110
ILLNESS AND DEATH 171
CONCLUDING NOTE 185
APPENDIX 187

PRIVATE LIFE

OF

DANIEL WEBSTER.

BIRTH AND BOYHOOD.

When it is remembered that Daniel Webster was considered the greatest intellectual character of his country, it is a striking coincidence that he should have been born in the shadow, as it were, of Mount Washington, and that his home and death-place was not only in full view of the landing-place of the Pilgrim fathers, but also on the margin of the Atlantic; as if Earth would commemorate his birth, History his deeds, and Ocean claim the privilege of floating his name to the remotest nations of the earth.

The ancestors of Daniel Webster came originally from Scotland, and his father, grandfather, and great-grandfather were named Ebenezer, and were descendants of Thomas Webster, who was one of the earliest settlers of New Hampshire. His father was a person of large and stalwart form, of swarthy complexion, and remarkable features. He was born and spent his youth upon a farm; served as a ranger in the famous company of Major Robert Rogers, and as a captain under General John Stark, during the Revolutionary war; was for several years a member of the Legislature of New Hampshire; and died while performing with honor the duties of judge of the Court of Common Pleas. He was not only a man of superior intellect, but was distinguished for his strong and indomitable will—a characteristic which his distinguished son rightfully inherited. He was a Federalist in politics; and it is related of him that he was once taken suddenly ill while passing through a village which was noted for its Democracy, and that, supposing that he was about to die, he beseeched his physician to remove him as soon as possible out of the place, giving, as a reason for his great anxiety, that "he was born a Federalist, had lived a Federalist, and could not die in any but a Federalist town." Mr. Webster's mother was Abigail Eastman, a lady of Welsh extraction, and of superior intellect. She was the second wife of her husband, and the mother of five children—two boys, Daniel and Ezekiel, and three daughters.

Daniel Webster was born on the 18th day of January, 1782, in the town of Salisbury, Merrimack county, then Hillsborough, New Hampshire. The site of the house is two and a half miles from the beautiful Merrimack River, and in the immediate vicinity of that where his father built the first log-cabin ever seen in this section of country, and at a time when, between his residence and the borders of Canada, there was not a single human habitation, excepting the Indian's wigwam. The house in question is not now standing; but the engraving which ornaments this volume is from a drawing correctly representing it, as it appeared only a few years ago, and is the only portrait of the place which ever received the approbation of Mr. Webster.* It was a good specimen of the more elegant farm-houses of the day, one story high, heavily timbered, clapboarded, with rather a pointed roof, one chimney in the centre, one front door, with a window on either side, three windows at each end, four rooms on the ground floor, and an addition in the rear for a kitchen. It fronted the south; a picturesque well-curb and sweep stood near the eastern extremity, and over the whole a mammoth elm-tree extended its huge arms, as if to protect the spot from sacrilege. In the rear, on a hillside, was a spacious barn, and a partially wooded pasture; the prospect immediately in front was enlivened by a rude bridge, spanning a lovely little stream, and bounded by a lofty hill, upon which is still standing the church where Mr. Webster was baptized; while in a southwesterly direction was presented a full view of the noble mountain called *Kearsage*, which holds the same rank among its brother hills that Mr. Webster was acknowledged to hold among men. The house was the centre of a tract of one hundred and sixty acres of land, which still belongs to the Webster family. Though the birth-place itself has disappeared, the waters of the well are still as pure and sparkling, and the leaves of the elm as luxuriant, as when they quenched the thirst and delighted the eyes of the infant statesman, some seventy years ago, and in their perennial nature are emblematic of the great name with which they are associated. And it was to this spot, and especially the

* The very good wood-cuts inserted in this volume were executed by Messrs. Lossing and Barritt.

log-cabin, that Mr. Webster alluded, when, in a speech delivered at Saratoga in 1840, he uttered the following touching words: "I make to it an annual visit. I carry my children to it, to teach them the hardships endured by the generations which have gone before them. I love to dwell on the tender recollections, the kindred ties, the early affections, and the touching narratives and incidents, which mingle with all I know of this primitive family abode. I weep to think that none of those who inhabited it are now living; and if ever I am ashamed of it, or if I ever fail in affectionate veneration for him who reared it, and defended it against savage violence and destruction, cherished all the domestic virtues beneath its roof, and, through the fire and blood of a seven years' Revolutionary war, shrunk from no danger, no toil, no sacrifice, to serve his country, and to raise his children to a better condition than his own, may my name, and the name of my posterity, be blotted forever from the memory of mankind."

Mr. Webster was first taught the letters of the alphabet by his mother, and, because of his feebleness when a child, was ever treated by her with partial kindness. From her lips, also, were first received the vital truths of the Bible, and the first copy of the sacred Volume which he ever owned was presented to him by his mother. Another tribute, and a most exalted one, is this fact, to the faithfulness of woman. The one in question is remembered, and always spoken of in New Hampshire, as a woman not only of superior intellect, but of the warmest affections, and remarkably beautiful. She lived for her husband and children, never thinking of herself, and was venerated by all who knew her ; and it is said that, when her son Daniel had attained his tenth year, she prophesied that he would become eminent ; and when she died, that son was indeed a member of Congress.

The first school-house into which Mr. Webster ever entered was built of logs, and not a vestige of it now remains, though the spot is marked by a still flourishing butternut-tree. It was located about half a mile from his father's house, and, as he only attended during the winter, it was pleasant to the writer to stand upon this now classic ground, and imagine the boy Daniel tramping on his way to school, carrying in one hand a little tin pail with his dinner, and in the other his spelling-book. The men who had the honor of first teaching in a public manner this favorite of fortune were Thomas Chase and James Tappan. The latter person is still living, at an advanced age, in Gloucester, Massachusetts. It may be well supposed that this veteran schoolmaster feels a deep affection and a great pride in his famous pupil. In 1851, he addressed a letter to Mr. Webster about the times of old, which drew forth the following letter, containing a bank-bill for fifty dollars, more, probably, than the old gentleman ever received for a winter's teaching in "New Salisbury."

"Washington, February 26th, 1851.

"Master Tappan,

"I thank you for your letter, and am rejoiced to know that you are among the living. I remember you perfectly well as a teacher of my infant years. I suppose my mother must have taught me to read very early, as I have never been able to recollect the time when I could not read the Bible. I think Master Chase was my earliest schoolmaster, probably when I was three or four years old. Then came Master Tappan. You boarded at our house, and sometimes, I think, in the family of Mr. Benjamin Sanborn, our neighbor, the lame man. Most of those whom you knew in 'New Salisbury' have gone to their graves. Mr. John Sanborn, the son of Benjamin, is yet living, and is about your age. Mr. John Colby, who married my eldest sister, Susannah, is also living. On the 'North Road' is Mr. Benjamin Pettingil. I think of none else among the living whom you would probably remember. You have, indeed, lived a checkered life. I hope you have been able to bear prosperity with meekness, and adversity with patience. These things are all ordered for us far better than we could order them for ourselves. We may pray for our daily bread; we may pray for the forgiveness of sins; we may pray to be kept from temptation, and that the kingdom of God may come, in us, and in all men, and his will every where be done. Beyond this we hardly know for what good to supplicate the Divine mercy. Our heavenly Father knoweth what we have need of better than we know ourselves, and we are sure that his eye and his loving-kindness are upon us and around us every moment.

"I thank you again, my good old schoolmaster, for your kind letter, which has awakened many sleeping recollections; and, with all good wishes, I remain, your friend and pupil, DANIEL WEBSTER.

"MR. JAMES TAPPAN."

In the month of July last a correspondent of the "Boston Transcript" wrote from Gloucester as follows: "Considerable interest has been excited here by the intelligence of the threatened difficulty with Great Britain, in consequence of the measures that have been taken by that government to exclude our fishermen from certain valuable fishing-grounds on the northeastern coast. Gloucester is largely interested in this question. Of some eighty thousand barrels of mackerel which she brings in, upward of sixty thousand are taken from grounds from which they are now to be excluded. Mr. Webster is confidently looked to in this juncture to ward off this threatened calamity from a most deserving and enterprising class of our fellow-citizens.

"The mention of Mr. Webster reminds me that I met on the piazza of the Pavilion last evening the venerable Mr. Tappan, now a resident of this town, and who was one of the earliest instructors of Daniel Webster and his brother Ezekiel. Master Tappan, as he is called, is now in his eighty-sixth year, somewhat infirm, but with his intellectual faculties bright and vivid, especially on the subject of his old pupil, whom he esteems the foremost man of his times, and in whose fame he takes a justifiable pride.

"'Daniel was always the brightest boy in the school,' said Master Tappan, 'and Ezekiel the next; but Daniel was much quicker at his studies than his brother. He would learn more in five minutes than another boy in five hours. One Saturday, I remember, I held up a handsome new jack-knife to the scholars, and said, the boy who would commit to memory the greatest number of verses in the

Bible by Monday morning should have it. Many of the boys did well; but when it came to Daniel's turn to recite, I found that he had committed so much that, after hearing him repeat some sixty or seventy verses, I was obliged to give up, he telling me that there were several chapters yet that he had learned. Daniel got that jack-knife. Ah! sir, he was remarkable even as a boy; and I told his father he would do God's work injustice if he did not send both Daniel and Ezekiel to college. The old man said he couldn't well afford it; but I told him he must, and he finally did. And didn't they both justify my good opinion? Well, gentlemen, I am an old man, and too much given to talk, perhaps. Well, good-by! Beautiful place this! Beautiful sea-view—and the air, how soft and refreshing! But I must leave it all soon, gentlemen. I have been suffering from the asthma for fifteen years, and it is now worse than ever. God is calling us all home—some sooner, some later—for me it must needs be soon. But, good-by! Enjoy yourselves in this delightful air. Good-by!'

"And the old gentleman tottered away, after a monologue almost verbatim such as I have recorded. It seems to be the one sunny spot in his old age to talk of his old pupil, and to expatiate on his greatness as a statesman, as an orator, and as a lawyer. Master Tappan alluded to the news in regard to the threatened difficulty with Great Britain on account of the northeastern fisheries, but confidently remarked, 'Daniel will settle it all, so that we shall hold our own, and have no trouble. They couldn't get along at all at Washington without Daniel. The country won't get into a scrape, while it has the benefit of *his* pilotage, be sure of that.' "

The above was read to Mr. Webster, and in less than an hour afterward the original of the following letter, which contained a remittance of twenty dollars, was on its way to gladden the heart of the old schoolmaster:

"Boston, July 20th, 1852.

"MASTER TAPPAN,

"I learn with much pleasure, through the public press, that you continue to enjoy life, with mental faculties bright and vivid, although you have arrived at a very advanced age, and are somewhat infirm. I came to-day from the very spot in which you taught me;* and to me a most delightful spot it is. The river and the hills are as beautiful as ever, but the graves of my father and mother, and brothers and sisters, and early friends, gave it to me something of the appearance of a city of the dead. But let me not repine. You have lived long, and my life is already not short, and we have both much to be thankful for. Two or three persons are yet living, who, like myself, were brought up *sub tua ferula*. They remember 'Master Tappan.'

"And now, my good old master, receive a renewed tribute of affectionate regard from your grateful pupil, with his wishes and prayers for your happiness in all that remains to you in this life, and more especially for your participation hereafter in the durable riches of righteousness. DANIEL WEBSTER."

* This was Mr. Webster's last visit to his birth-place.

Near the site of the house where Mr. Webster was born, and in the bed of a little brook, are the remains of an old mill, which once stood in a dark glen, and was there surrounded with a majestic forest which covered the neighboring hills. The mill was a source of income to his father, and he kept it in operation till near the close of his life. To that mill, Daniel, though a small boy, went daily, when not in school, to assist his father in sawing boards. He was apt in learning any thing useful, and soon became so expert in doing every thing required, that his services as an assistant were valuable. And oftentimes, after setting the saw and hoisting the gate, and while the saw was passing through the log, which occupied some ten minutes for each board, he was usually seen reading attentively the books in the way of biography and history, which he was permitted to take from the house.

There, in that old saw-mill, surrounded by forests, in the midst of the noise which such a mill made, and this, too, without neglecting his task, he made himself familiar with the most remarkable events recorded by the pen of history, and with the lives and characters of the most celebrated persons of antiquity. What he read there has never been forgotten. So tenacious was his memory, that he has been able, within the last few years, to recite long narratives out of the old books upon which he then feasted, and which he had not subsequently perused. The solitude of the scene, the absence of every thing to divert his attention, the simplicity of his occupation, the taciturn and thoughtful manner of his father, all favored the process of transplanting every great idea found in those books to his own fresh, fruitful, and vigorous mind. Few other scenes of his boyhood are as interesting as the site of this old mill.

At this period of his life it was, too, that his eyes first fell upon the Constitution of the United States, of which he subsequently became the *chief expounder and defender.* And what is truly remarkable, is the fact that this particular copy was printed upon an imported cotton pocket handkerchief, according to a fashion of the time, which he chanced to stumble upon in a country store, and for which he paid, out of his own pocket, all the money he had, twenty-five cents. The evening of the day on which he obtained the document was wholly devoted to its close and attentive perusal, while seated before the fire, and by the side of his father and mother. What dreamer, on that night, in the wildest flights of his imagination, could have seen the result of that accident, or marked out the future career of that New Hampshire boy?

But with all this earnestness of character, there was closely connected a frolicsome disposition, which, for its smartness as well as harmlessness, it is pleasant to contemplate. Of the many anecdotes which tend to illustrate his love of fun, the following are worth mentioning:

Daniel and his brother Ezekiel, when boys, were really devoted to the pursuits of agriculture, but the following story is current in the vicinity of their birth-place. Their father had given them directions to perform a specific labor during his temporary absence from home, but on his return at night, he found the labor unperformed, and, with a frown upon his face, questioned the boys in regard to their idleness. "What have you been doing, Ezekiel?" said the father. "Nothing, sir," was the reply. "Well, Daniel, what have *you* been doing?" "*Helping Zeke, sir.*"

On another occasion, Daniel was put to mowing. He made bad work of it. His scythe was sometimes in the ground, and sometimes over the tops of all the grass. He complained to his father that his scythe was not hung right. Various attempts were made to hang it better, but with no success. His father told him, at length, he might hang it to suit himself; and he therefore hung it upon a tree, and said, "There, that's just right." His father laughed, and told him to let it hang there.

When Daniel and Ezekiel were boys together, they had frequent literary disputes, and on one occasion, after they had retired to bed, they entered into a squabble about a certain passage in one of their school-books, and having risen to examine some of the authorities in their possession, they set their bed-clothes on fire and nearly burned up their father's dwelling. On being questioned the next morning in regard to the accident, Daniel remarked, "*That they were in pursuit of light, but got more than they wanted.*"

The father of these brothers used to speak of them with great kindness, but dwelt principally upon the qualifications of Ezekiel; and when questioned by a friend as to his reasons for so doing, he replied, "Ezekiel is a bashful boy, who needs a word to be said of him; but Daniel, I warrant you, will take care of himself."

The father was very strict in all religious observances, and required, among other things, that his sons should go every Sunday to church, though the distance was about four miles. Daniel complained of the hardship, for he must needs walk all the way. His father said to him,

"I see Deacon True's boys there every Sunday regularly, and have never heard of their complaining."

"Ah! yes," replied Daniel; "the deacon's boys live half the way there, and of course have only half as far to walk."

"Well," said his father, "you may get up in the morning, dress yourself, and run up to Deacon True's, and go with them; then you will have no further to walk than they do."

The logic of his father was conclusive, for he never considered it a hardship to run up to Deacon True's to play with the boys, and that the hardship, if any, lay beyond the deacon's residence. On every future pleasant Sabbath, therefore, Daniel was found at church, notwithstanding the distance.

And now we have an anecdote to record, going to show the existence of an innate eloquence. When he was about seven years of age, his father kept a house of public entertainment, where the teamsters, who traveled on the road, were in the habit of obtaining a dinner, and feeding their horses; and it is said that the incipient orator and statesman frequently entertained his father's guests by reading aloud some of the Psalms of David, to the great delight of his rustic listeners. Indeed, it was customary for the teamsters to remark, as they pulled up their horses before the Webster tavern, "Come, let's go in and hear a Psalm from *Dan Webster!*" Even at that time, his voice was deep, rich, and musical. The identical dwelling alluded to above is still standing, and it was only a few months ago, when Mr. Webster, bending under the weight of years and a painful illness, sat with the writer upon its little porch, and descanted with streaming eyes upon the various events associated with his "boyhood's home."

COLLEGE DAYS.

MR. WEBSTER'S advantages of early education were exceedingly slender, for he worked on the farm in summer, and went to school only in the winter. The principal district school that he attended was three miles from his father's residence, and his pathway thither was often through deep snows. When fourteen years old, he spent a few months at Phillips' Academy, Exeter, enjoying the tuition and kindly counsels of Dr. Benjamin Abbot. He mastered the principles and philosophy of the English grammar in less than four months, when he immediately commenced the study of the Latin language, and his first lessons therein were recited to the late *Joseph Stevens Buckminster*, who was at that time a tutor in the academy. Here he was first called upon to "speak in public on the stage," and the effort was a failure; for the moment he began he became embarrassed, and burst into tears. He could repeat psalms to a few teamsters at the age of seven, but could not address an assembly when twice that age. His antipathy to public declamation was insurmountable; and in bearing testimony to this fact, he once uttered the following words: "I believe I made tolerable progress in most branches which I attended to while in this school, but there was one thing I could not do—I could not make a declamation; I could not speak before the school. The kind and excellent Buckminster sought especially to persuade me to perform the exercise of declamation, like other boys, but I could not do it. Many a piece did I commit to memory, and recite and rehearse in my own room, over and over again; yet, when the day came when the school collected to hear the declamations, when my name was called, and I saw all eyes turned to my seat, I could not raise myself from it. Sometimes the instructors frowned; sometimes they smiled. Mr. Buckminster always pressed and entreated, most winningly, that I would venture, venture only once. But I never could command sufficient resolution."

A few days after Mr. Webster had entered Exeter academy, he returned to his boarding-house one evening in a very desponding mood, and told his friends there that the city boys in the academy were constantly laughing at him, because he was at the foot of his class, and had come from the back-woods. His friends endeavored to cheer him by explaining the regulations of the school, and telling him that the boys would soon get tired of their unhandsome conduct, and that he ought to show himself above their foolishness. Mr. Nicholas Emerey, who was then an assistant tutor in the academy, was also made acquainted with young Webster's troubles, and, as he had the management of the second or lower class, he treated his desponding pupil with marked kindness, and particularly urged upon him to think of nothing but his books, and that all would yet come out bright. This advice was heeded; and at the end of the first quarter Mr. Emerey mustered his class in a line, and formally took the arm of young Webster, and marched him from the foot to the extreme head of the class, exclaiming, in the mean while, that this was his proper position. Such an event had for many days been anticipated, but when actually accomplished the remainder of the class were surprised and chagrined.

This triumph greatly encouraged the boy Daniel, and he renewed his efforts with his books. He did not doubt but that there were many boys in the class as smart as himself, if not smarter; and he looked with some anxiety to the summing up of the second quarter. The day arrived, the class was mustered, and Mr. Emerey stood before it, when the breathless silence was broken by these words: "Daniel Webster, gather up your books and take down your cap."

The boy obeyed, and, thinking that he was about to be expelled from school, was sorely troubled about the cause of the calamity. The teacher saw this, but soon dispelled the illusion, for he continued: "Now, sir, you will please report yourself to the teacher of the *first class;* and you, young gentlemen, will take an affectionate leave of your class-mate, *for you will never see him again.*" That teacher is still living, is a man of distinction, and has ever been a warm friend of his fortunate pupil.

In his fifteenth year he was privileged to spend some months with one of the more prominent clergymen of the day, the Rev. Samuel Woods, who lived at Boscawen, and prepared boys for college at one dollar a week, for tuition and board. During his stay with Dr. Woods, he was apparently very neglectful of his academic duties, but never failed to perform all his intellectual tasks with great credit. On one occasion the reverend tutor thought proper to give his scholar Daniel a scolding for spending too much of his time upon the hills and along the streams, hunting and fishing, but still complimented him for his smartness. The task assigned to him for his next recitation was one hundred lines of Virgil; and as he knew that his master had an engagement on the following morning, an idea occurred to him, and he spent the entire night poring over his books. The recitation hour finally arrived, and the scholar acquitted himself of his hundred lines and received the tutor's approbation. "But I have a few more lines that I can recite," said the boy Daniel. "Well, let us have them," replied the doctor; and forthwith the boy reeled off another hundred lines. "Very remarkable," said the doctor; "you are indeed a smart boy." "But I have another," said the scholar, "and five hundred of them, if you please." The doctor was, of course, astonished, but, as he bethought him of his engagement, he begged to be excused, and added, "You may have the whole day, Dan, for pigeon shooting."

It was while on their way to Mr. Woods, by-the-way, that Mr. Webster's father for the first time opened to him the design of sending him to college. The advantages of such an education were a privilege to which he had never aspired in his most ambitious moments. "I remember," he once said, "the very hill which we were ascending, through deep snows, in a New England sleigh, when my father made known this promise to me. I could not speak.

How could he, I thought, with so large a family, and in such narrow circumstances, think of incurring so great an expense for me. A warm glow ran all over me, and I laid my head on my father's shoulder and wept."

When Mr. Webster was a pupil of Dr. Woods, his father wrote him a letter, requesting that he would come to Elm's Farm to assist him in haying for a few days. He packed up his bundle of clothes and obeyed orders. On the morning after his arrival home, the boy went to work in the field, while the father visited a neighboring town on business. About eleven o'clock the boy came to his mother and told her he was very tired, that his hands were blistered, and that he could not work any longer. The kind mother excused her son, as a matter of course, and all was well. About an hour after dinner, however, young Daniel had tackled up the family horse, placed two of his sisters in a wagon, and taken his departure for a famous whortleberry hill, where he spent the rest of the day scampering over the rocks like a young deer. His father returned at night, and having questioned Daniel and his mother about the amount of work he had performed, and heard the particulars, he laughed, and sent him to bed. The next morning, after breakfast, the father handed his hopeful son his bundle of clothes, and, with a smiling countenance, significantly pointed toward Boscawen, and the boy disappeared. As he left the house a neighbor saw him, and laughed.

"Where are you going, Dan?" said he.

"Back to school," replied Daniel.

"I thought it would be so," added the neighbor, and

uttered another quiet laugh; and back to the academic shades returned the incipient statesman.

The neighbor alluded to above was Thomas W. Thompson, who subsequently became a representative in Congress, and who, from the beginning, conceived a high idea of Mr. Webster's future eminence.

As has already been intimated, he was only a few months in preparing himself for college, and during that brief period he commenced and mastered the study of Greek, so that his tutor was wont to remark that other boys required an entire year to accomplish the same end. Of all his father's children Daniel Webster was, as a boy, the sickliest and most slender; and one of his half-brothers, who was somewhat of a wag, frequently took pleasure in remarking that "Dan was sent to school because he was not fit for any thing else, and that he might know as much as the other boys." Even from his earliest boyhood he was an industrious reader of standard authors, and previous to his entering college his favorite books were Addison's Spectator, Butler's Hudibras, Pope's translation of Homer, and the Essay on Man, the last of which he committed to memory; and though he has never looked it through since his fifteenth year, he is at the present time able to recite most of it from beginning to end. He was particularly fond, too, of the Bible, of Shakspeare, and of devotional poetry, and simply as a pleasure he committed to memory many of the Psalms and Hymns of Dr. Watts. An English translation of Don Quixote was another of his favorite books, the power of which over his imagination he has described as having been very great. He studied with interest both Cicero and Virgil, but he was particularly partial to Cicero. As he advanced in years, he added Sallust, Cæsar, Horace, and Demosthenes to the list of classic authors which he made it his business, as it was his pleasure, to master; hence it is not surprising that the productions of his own mind should be distinguished for their refined and classic elegance.

Mr. Webster went through college in a manner that was highly creditable to himself and gratifying to his friends. He graduated at Dartmouth in 1801, and though it was universally believed that he ought to have received, and would receive the valedictory, that honor was not conferred upon him, but upon one whose name has since passed into forgetfulness. The ill-judging faculty of the college, however, bestowed upon him a diploma, but instead of pleasing, this commonplace compliment only disgusted him, and at the conclusion of the commencement exercises the disappointed youth asked a number of his classmates to accompany him to the green behind the college, where, in their presence, he deliberately *tore up* his honorary document, and threw it to the winds, exclaiming, "My industry may make me a great man, but this miserable parchment can not!" and immediately mounting his horse, departed for home.

While at college he was faithful to all his regular duties, but devoted much of his time to general reading, especially English literature and history. He took part in a weekly newspaper by contributing to it an occasional article; and also delivered an occasional address. Those who would like to read his first printed oration, which was delivered to the people of Hanover, are referred to the choice collections of American antiquarians; and it is to be regretted that it did not appear in the late edition of his works. Suffice it to say, that it proves his bosom to have been, even at that early day, full of patriotism, and that in his youth the seeds of his noblest sentiments had taken deep root. The title-page was as follows: "An Oration, pronounced at Hanover, N. H., the 4th of July, 1800, being the twenty-fourth Anniversary of American Independence. By Daniel Webster, Member of the Junior Class, Dartmouth College.

"Do thou, great Liberty, inspire our souls,
And make our lives in thy possession happy,
Or our deaths glorious in thy just defense.—ADDISON.

Published by request, and printed at Hanover, by Moses Davis."

On his return home from college, the one great thought which occupied his mind was that his brother Ezekiel should also receive a liberal education. But his father was poor, and how could this result be attained? "By keeping school," said he to himself, "and this shall be the first business of my life." No sooner had this idea occurred to him than he sought an opportunity to broach it to his much-loved brother. The boys slept together, and he did this on their next retiring to bed. Ezekiel was surprised, but delighted, for he had long felt a yearning desire to acquire a college education. The trying circumstances of the family were, of course, all discussed, and as they thought of the strong affection which existed between them, and of the "clouds and shadows" which enveloped the future, they talked and talked, and wept many and bitter tears, so that when morning came it found the brothers still wakeful, troubled, and unhappy, but yet determined and hopeful. On that very day, the youth Daniel left his home to become a country schoolmaster, while Ezekiel hastened to place himself under the preparatory tuition of the Rev. Samuel Woods, as his brother had done before him.

The place where Mr. Webster spent the most of his time as a schoolmaster was Fryeburg, in the State of Maine. He had been invited thither by a friend of his father, who was acquainted with the circumstances of the family. His school was quite large, and his salary $350, to which he added a considerable sum by devoting his evenings to copying deeds, in the office of the county recorder, at twenty-five cents per deed. He also found time during this period to go through with his first reading of Blackstone's Commentaries, and other substantial works, which have been so good a foundation to his after fame.

The writer once questioned Mr. Webster as to his personal appearance when officiating as a pedagogue, and his reply was, "Long, slender, pale, and all eyes; indeed, I went by the name of *all eyes* the country round."

During the summer of 1851, when returning from a visit to the White Mountains, accompanied by his son Fletcher, he went out of his way to spend a day or two in the town of Fryeburg. He revisited, after the lapse of half a century, the office of the Recorder of Deeds, and there found and exhibited to his son two large bound volumes of his own handwriting, the sight of which was, of course, suggestive of manifold emotions. The son testifies that the penmanship is neat and elegant; and the father that the *ache* is not yet out of those fingers which so much writing caused them. In one of the volumes was found a respectful and affectionate vote of thanks and good-will for the services he had performed.

It is said by those who knew Mr. Webster at Fryeburg, that his only recreation, while a school-teacher, was derived from trout fishing, and that his Wednesday and Saturday afternoons were almost invariably spent wandering alone, with rod in hand, and a copy of Shakspeare in his pocket, along the wild and picturesque brooks of that section of country.

As Dartmouth College gave Mr. Webster the greater part of his classical education, it ought to be mentioned how it was that he was subsequently enabled to make an adequate return to that institution. In 1816, according to the clear narrative of Samuel L. Knapp, the Legislature of New Hampshire, believing that the right of altering or amending the charter of this college, which had been granted by the king previous to the Revolution, was vested in them by the Constitution of the state, proceeded to enlarge and improve it. This act was not accepted nor assented to by the trustees of Dartmouth College, and they refused to submit to it any further than they were compelled to do so by the necessities of the case. The new institution, called by the act of the Legislature, "The Dartmouth University," went into operation, as far as existing circumstances would permit. There were two presidents, two sets of professors in the same village, and, of course, no good fellowship between them. The students generally took side with the college party, a few only going over to the university. It was a very uncomfortable state of things. The faculty of both institutions were highly respectable, and capable of building up any literary and scientific seminary, had they been under different auspices. The lawyers were consulted, and the most distinguished of them, Smith, Mason, and Webster, were of the opinion that the act of the Legislature of New Hampshire was unconstitutional, and of course not valid. It was conceded that there were many difficulties in the case; but it was indispensable that the question should be decided, that one of the institutions might survive the quarrel. The records, charter, and the evidence of the college property, were in the hands of the new treasurer, and an action of trover was brought by the trustees of Dartmouth College to recover them. The facts were agreed on. The question, "Whether the acts of the Legislature of New Hampshire, of the 27th of June, and of the 16th and 18th of December, 1816, are valid and binding on the rights of the plaintiffs, without their acceptance or assent?"

It was a great constitutional question. The people of Massachusetts took as deep an interest in it as those of New Hampshire. The cause was ably argued before the Supreme Court of New Hampshire, and the opinion of the court was given by Chief-justice Richardson, in favor of the validity and constitutionality of the acts of the Legislature, and judgment was accordingly entered up for the defendant. Thereupon a writ of error was sued out by the plaintiffs in the original suit, and the cause removed to the Supreme Court of the United States. In March, 1818, the cause was argued before all the judges by Mr. Webster and Mr. Hopkinson for the plaintiffs, and by Mr. Holmes and Mr. Wirt for the defendant in error. The anxiety of the parties, the great constitutional principle involved, the deep interest felt by every lawyer in the country in the decision of the question, gave more notoriety to the cause than to any ever brought before that august tribunal. Some were apprehensive that the court would evade the question in some way or other. Mr. Webster had no such fears. He knew the judges well enough to believe, that while they were not anxious to meet constitutional questions, whenever they were fully brought before them, the subject would be most solemnly considered and as fearlessly decided. The question was argued on both sides with great ability. The counsel were men of research, and their reputations were in the case; for it was well known, whatever way it was decided, it would form a leading case. Mr. Webster came to his work fully possessed of all the views that could be taken of the subject, and he sustained and increased by this argument the reputation he had acquired as a profound constitutional lawyer. Chiefly through his acknowledged instrumentality, the judgment of the State Court was reversed, the acts of the Legislature declared null and void, as being unconstitutional. The university disappeared; the college rose with new vigor, and the people of New Hampshire acquiesced in the decision, and a great portion of the thinking people of the country considered it as a new proof of the wisdom and strength of the Constitution of the United States.

EARLY LEGAL CAREER.

Mr. Webster was admitted to the practice of the law, in Boston, in 1805, and was first introduced to the public as a lawyer by the distinguished person with whom he had chiefly studied his profession, Christopher Gore. After practicing in Boston about one year, his father died, and he returned to his paternal home. In 1807 he was admitted to practice in the courts of New Hampshire, and took up his residence at Portsmouth, where he remained about nine years.

It ought to be mentioned in this place, however, that, just before entering upon his Boston practice, he was tendered the vacant clerkship of the Court of Common Pleas for the county of Hillsborough, New Hampshire, of which his father was one of the judges, and the appointment had been bestowed upon his son by his colleagues as a token of personal regard. The office was worth some fifteen hundred dollars, which in those days, and that section of country, was equal to the salary of Secretary of State at the present time. Delighted with this realization of his most sanguine hopes, the father hastened to communicate the joyful intelligence to his son.

That son was then a student in the office of Christopher Gore, in Boston. He received the news with sensations of gladness that he had never before experienced. With a loud, throbbing heart he announced the tidings to his legal counselor and friend, and, to his utter astonishment, that far-seeing and sagacious man expressed, in the most pointed manner, his utter disapprobation of the proposed change in his pursuits. "But my father is poor, and I wish to make him comfortable in his old age," replied the student.

"That may all be," continued Mr. Gore, "but you should think of the future more than of the present. Become once a clerk and you will always be a clerk, with no prospect of attaining a higher position. Go on and finish your legal studies; you are, indeed, poor, but there are greater evils than poverty; live on no man's favor; what bread you do eat, let it be the bread of independence; pursue your profession; make yourself useful to the world and formidable to your enemies, and you will have nothing to fear."

The student listened attentively to these sound arguments, and had the good sense to appreciate them. His determination was immediately made; and now came the dreaded business of advising his father as to his intended course. He felt that it would be a difficult task to satisfy him of its propriety, and he therefore determined to go home without delay, and give him in full all the reasons of his conduct.

In three days, in spite of the inclemency of the weather, for it was winter, he had reached the dwelling on Elms Farm. According to his own account, he arrived there in the evening, and found his father sitting before the fire. He received him with manifest joy. He looked feebler than he had ever appeared, but his countenance lighted up on seeing his clerk stand before him in good health and spirits. He lost no time in alluding to the great appointment; said how spontaneously it had been made, how kindly the chief justice proposed it, and with what unanimity all assented. During this speech, it can be well imagined how embarrassed Mr. Webster felt, compelled, as he thought, from a conviction of duty, to disappoint his father's sanguine expectations. Nevertheless, he commanded his countenance and voice, so as to reply in a sufficiently assured manner. He spoke gayly about the office; expressed his great obligation to their honors, and his intention to write them a most respectful letter; if he could have consented to record any body's judgments, he should have been proud to have recorded their honors, &c., &c. He proceeded in this strain till his father exhibited signs of amazement, it having occurred to him, finally, that his son might all the while be serious. "Do you intend to decline this office?" he said, at length. "Most certainly," replied his son. "I can not think of doing otherwise. I mean to use my tongue in the courts, not my pen; to be an actor, not a register of other men's actions."

For a moment Judge Webster seemed angry. He rocked his chair slightly; a flash went over his eye, softened by age, but even then black as jet, but it soon disappeared, and his countenance regained its usual serenity. "Well, my son," said Judge Webster, finally, "your mother always said that you would come to something or nothing—become a somebody or a nobody; it is now settled that you are to be a nobody." In a few days the student returned to Boston, and the subject was never afterward mentioned in the family.

Within six months after Mr. Webster had declined the county court clerkship, he was, even as a student in Mr. Gore's office, remarkably successful in accumulating money for his legal services, and being aware of the fact that his father was considerably embarrassed in his circumstances, he resolved to go home and liquidate all the pending claims. He arrived at home ostensibly for a friendly visit. It was Saturday night, and he sought an early opportunity to have a private interview with his father. "Father, I am going to pay your debts," said he.

"Oh, my son, that can never be; you know not how numerous they are."

"But I can, and will, father; and that, too, before next Monday night."

On the Tuesday morning following, Judge Webster was a free man, and his son Daniel was on his return to Boston.

Mr. Webster practiced law in Portsmouth nearly nine years, and during that time one of his best friends, and also his most prominent competitor, was the distinguished Jeremiah Mason. On one occasion a gentleman called upon the former for the purpose of securing his services in a lawsuit; but Mr. Webster was compelled to decline the engagement, but recommended his client to Mr. Mason.

"What do you think of the abilities of Mr. Mason?" said the gentleman.

"I think him second to no man in the country," replied Mr. Webster.

The gentleman called upon Mr. Mason, and having secured his promise of assistance, he thought he would gratify his curiosity, and therefore questioned him as to his opinion of Mr. Webster. "He's the very devil, in any case whatsoever," replied Mr. Mason; "and if he's against you, I beg to be excused."

Mr. Webster, who subsequently met Pinkney, and Wirt, and Emmet at the bar, recently said that he never feared any of them so much as Jeremiah Mason.

The first meeting of Mr. Webster with Jeremiah Mason was in a criminal trial. A noted person, belonging to the Democratic party, had been indicted for counterfeiting, and it was deemed particularly important that he should be acquitted. Mr. Mason stood foremost among his professional brethren, and was of course employed to defend the accused. When the trial came on, the Attorney General happened to be absent, whereupon Mr. Webster was delegated to conduct the prosecution for the state. Mr. Mason came into court, and conducted himself somewhat after the manner of Goliath; but when Mr. Webster, like another David (to use the language of a contemporary), "came down upon his distinguished opponent like a shower of hail," Mr. Mason was astonished, and began to tremble for the fate of his client. It so happened, however, that a Democratic jury acquitted their friend; but Mr. Mason subsequently expressed himself as having being struck with the high, open, and manly ground taken by Mr. Webster, not resorting to technicalities, but sticking to the main points of the law and the facts, and at that early period prophesied that his future public career would be particularly brilliant and useful.

In legal acquirements and logical skill, Jeremiah Mason and Jeremiah Smith, according to the Rev. John H. Morrison, were not the unworthy associates and antagonists of Daniel Webster; while, in the combination of gifts which make the commanding orator, he stood with them, as he had done every where else, like Mount Washington among the other mountains of New England. Mr. Smith often said that in single qualities he had known men superior to Mr. Webster; that Hamilton had more original genius; Ames greater quickness of imagination; that Marshall, Parsons, and Dexter were as remarkable for logical strength; but that in the union of high intellectual qualities he had known no man whom he thought his equal.

Among the New Hampshire anecdotes which Mr. Webster was in the habit of occasionally narrating to his friends was the following, which we give the substance of in nearly his own words:

"Soon after commencing the practice of my profession at Portsmouth, I was waited on by an old acquaintance of my father's, resident in an adjacent county, who wished to engage my professional services. Some years previous, he had rented a farm, with the clear understanding that he could purchase it, after the expiration of his lease, for one thousand dollars. Finding the said productive, he soon determined to own it, and, as he laid aside money for the purchase, he was prompted to improve what he felt certain he would possess. But his landlord finding the property greatly increased in value, coolly refused to receive the one thousand dollars, when in due time it was presented; and when his extortionate demand of double that sum was refused, he at once brought an action of ejectment. The man had but the one thousand dollars, and an unblemished reputation, yet I willingly undertook his case.

"The opening argument of the plaintiff's attorney left me little ground for hope. He stated that he could prove that my client hired the farm, but there was not a word in the lease about the sale, nor was there a word spoken about the sale when the lease was signed, as he should prove by a witness. In short, his was a clear case, and I left the court-room at dinner-time with feeble hopes of success. By chance, I sat at table next a newly-commissioned militia officer, and a brother lawyer began to joke him about his lack of martial knowledge; 'Indeed,' he jocosely remarked, 'you should write down the orders, and get old W—— to beat them into your sconce, as I saw him this morning, with a paper in his hand, teaching something to young M—— in the court-house entry.'

"Can it be, I thought, that old W——, the plaintiff in the case, was instructing young M——, who was his reliable witness?

"After dinner the court was reopened, and M—— was put on the stand. He was examined by the plaintiff's counsel, and certainly told a clear, plain story, repudiating all knowledge of any agreement to sell. When he had concluded, the opposite counsel, with a triumphant glance, turned to me, and asked me if I was satisfied? 'Not quite,' I replied.

"I had noticed a piece of paper protruding from M——'s pocket, and hastily approaching him, I seized it before he had the least idea of my intention. 'Now,' I asked, 'tell me if this paper does not detail the story you have so clearly told, and is it not false?' The witness hung his head with shame; and when the paper was found to be what I had supposed, and in the very handwriting of old W——, he lost his case at once. Nay, there was such a storm of indignation against him that he soon removed to the West.

"Years afterward, visiting New Hampshire, I was the guest of my professional brethren at a public dinner; and toward the close of the festivities, I was asked if I would solve a great doubt by answering a question. 'Certainly.' 'Well, then, Mr. Webster, we have often wondered how you knew what was in M——'s pocket.'"

By way of showing the character of some of his fees while practicing law at Portsmouth, the following incident is worth recording: One of his clients, after gaining a certain suit, found himself unable to raise the necessary funds to pay his lawyer, and therefore insisted upon deeding to him a piece of land in a neighboring county. And so the matter rested for many years. Happening to be on a visit to this county at a subsequent period, he hunted out this land, and found an old woman living upon it alone, in an old house situated among rocks. He questioned the woman about the farm, and learned that it was the property of a lawyer named Webster, and that she was daily expecting him to come on and turn her out of doors. Whereupon he made himself known as the proprietor, gave her a word of consolation, with a present of fifty dollars, broke bread with her at her humble board, and took his departure. From that time to the present the place has been known as "Webster's Farm," and it is believed that up to the day of his death the idea of this possession had never entered his mind.

At the time that Mr. Webster quitted Portsmouth for Boston, he was doing the heaviest law business of any man in New Hampshire; he was retained in nearly all the important causes, and but seldom appeared as the junior counsel. His practice was chiefly in the Circuit Courts; and during the last six weeks of his labors, previous to his departure for Boston, his earnings amounted to only five hundred dollars. This was the result of a journey into every county in the state, and was really the primal cause of his removal to a wider sphere of action.

When Mr. Webster was practicing law in his native state, "riding the circuit" was a very different matter from what it now is, in this age of rail-roads. So extensive was his business, even at this period, that he was frequently compelled to journey from one place to another during the night. On one occasion, after a toilsome series of days and nights, he was journeying on horseback, as usual, along a lonely road, when he fell into a profound study upon the merits of the case he was compelled to attend to on the following morning. Long and tedious was the trial as it proceeded in the chamber of his brain, when, just as the jury was about to pronounce the verdict, a drop of water fell upon his hand, and lo! as the moon came out of a cloud, he found himself comfortably seated on his horse, which had sought a convenient standing-place under an old oak, as if determined that its master should enjoy the quiet nap which he so much needed. Thanks to the dew-drop, the journey was resumed, and the cause of the following day was satisfactorily settled.

It was in the year 1817 that Mr. Webster took up his permanent residence in Boston. During his career as a member of Congress, to which he was first elected in 1812, his legal and private interests had materially suffered, and he felt the need of a broader field than Portsmouth for his future action. He had already become identified, says Mr. Knapp, in his biography, with the interests of the New England metropolis, and the more opulent merchants doing business there were ready to employ him. Boston was then the residence of some of the first lawyers of the nation; such men, for example, as Dexter, Prescott, Otis, Sullivan, Shaw, Gorham, and Hubbard, and there seemed to be little room for another in the upper class of the legal fraternity; but Mr. Webster seemed to walk into this distinguished company like one who had a right to be there, and though many opened wide their eyes, none dared to question his right to be there. In a very few months his name appeared as senior counsel in many important causes, and he deported himself like one who was simply enjoying his birth-right. His practice was not confined to the county of Suffolk, but extended to the neighboring counties, and others in the interior of the state. His powers as an advocate and a lawyer were at once conceded, though some found fault with his manners at the bar as a little too severe and sharp; this, however, was soon forgotten in the admiration that every where followed him.

The people were always with him, and few had the hardihood to declare themselves his rivals.

As were his manners at the bar some thirty years ago, so were they through his life, whenever he appeared in a deliberative assembly. He began to state his points in a low voice, and in a slow, cool, cautious, and philosophical manner. If the case was of importance, he went on, hammering out, link by link, his chain of argument, with ponderous blows, leisurely inflicted; and, while thus at labor, you rather saw the sinews of the arm than the skill of the artist. It was in reply, however, that he came out in the majesty of intellectual grandeur, and poured forth the opulence of his mind; it was when the arrows of the enemy had hit him that he was all might and soul, and showered his words of weight and fire. His style of oratory was founded on no model, but was entirely his own. He dealt not with the fantastic and poetical, but with the matter-of-fact, every-day world, and the multifarious affairs of his fellow-men, extricating them from difficulties, and teaching them how to become happy. He never strove to dazzle, astonish, or confuse, but went on to convince and conquer by great but legitimate means. When he went out to battle, he went alone, trusting to no earthly arm but his own. He asked for no trophies but his own conquests; he looked not for the laurel of victory, but it was proffered to him by all, and bound his brow until he went out on some new exploit.

As Mr. Webster was a prominent politician for about forty years, it may gratify curiosity to know when and how he entered upon this important career. It was before he had attained his thirtieth year, when the times were stormy, and party spirit ran high in view of a war with Great Britain. He entered the field, says Mr. Knapp, like one who had made up his mind to be decided, firm, and straightforward in all his actions. No politician was ever more direct and bold, and he had nothing of the demagogue about him. Fully persuaded of the true course, he followed it with so much firmness and principle, that sometimes his serenity was taken by the furious and headstrong as apathy; but when a fair and legitimate opportunity offered, he came out with such strength and manliness that the doubting were satisfied and the complaining silenced. In the worst of times and the darkest hour, he had faith in the redeeming qualities of the people. They might be wrong, but he saw into their true character sufficiently to believe that they would never remain permanently in error. In some of his conversations upon the subject, he compared the people, in the management of the national affairs, to that of the sagacious and indefatigable raftsmen on his native Merrimack, who had falls and shoals to contend with in their course to the ocean—guiding fearlessly and skillfully over the former—between rocks and through breakers; and, when reaching the sand-banks, jumping off into the water, with lever, ax, and oar; and then, with pushing, cutting, and directing, made all rub and go to the astonishment of those looking on.

The first halo of political glory that hung around his brow was at a convention of the great spirits in the county of Rockingham, where he then resided, and such representatives from other counties as were sent to this convention, to take into consideration the state of the nation, and to mark out such a course for themselves as should be deemed advisable by the collected wisdom of those assembled. On this occasion an address with a string of resolutions were proposed for adoption, of which he was the author. They exhibited uncommon powers of intellect, and a profound knowledge of our national interests. He made a most powerful speech in support of these resolutions, portions of which were printed at the time, and much admired throughout the Union. From this time he belonged to the United States, and not to New Hampshire exclusively. Massachusetts also took as great an interest in his career as his native state. After the above *débût*, crowds gathered around him on every occasion that he appeared, and his speeches were invariably received with the most sincere and heartfelt applause.

ELMS FARM.

THE spot where Mr. Webster spent the greater part of his childhood and youth is known as the "Elms Farm," and is only about three miles from his birth-place. It contains one thousand acres, lies directly in a bend of the Merrimack, and is one of the finest farms in New Hampshire. It descended to his brother Ezekiel and himself after the death of their father in 1806, and though intrinsically of great value, yet to the admirer of the great and good in human intellect it must ever be a kind of Mecca, and possess a value not to be estimated by money. A portion of it is interval land, while the remainder comprehends a number of picturesque hills, from some of which may be seen the *White Mountains*, including the grand summit of *Mount Washington*, and between *Kearsage* and the *Ragged Mountains* the picturesque peak of *Ascutny*, in Vermont.

It is pre-eminently a grazing farm, and one of the meadow fields alone contains nearly one hundred acres, and as it is encircled and occasionally dotted with graceful elms, it presents a truly charming appearance; especially so during the haying season, when a score or two of men are wielding the scythe in a kind of cavalcade; or when, as in autumn, it is the pasturing ground of herds composed of the Devon, Ayrshire, and Hereford breeds of cattle.

Near the centre of the above field are the almost obliterated remains of a fort which links the farm with its early history, when this particular region was the frontier of the British colonies, and when the Indians, as the allies of the French, made it their chief business to destroy the pioneer inhabitants. The fort stood on a ridge of land south of the burying-ground, and the plow which passes over it at the present day frequently brings to light warlike memorials of the olden times. But a Sabbath peace now broods over the domain of the Webster family; the wilderness has indeed blossomed as the rose; the war-whoop has given place to the lowing of cattle, the bleating of sheep, and the tinkling of bells; and yet it is pleasant to know that the changes are not universal; for the same morning and evening atmospheres—the same healthful breezes—and the same loud singing birds, with the whip-powil, too, were recently there to make glad and to soothe the heart, in the evening as once in the morning of his days, of that great and good man who was born among these hills, and whose name has baptized them with a classic fame. One of the last Indian murders committed in New Hampshire, that of Mrs. Call, was on this estate. Here yet remain the cellar of her habitation, and the visible plot of her garden, where her husband raised his Indian corn one hundred years ago, and down to the period of Mr. Webster's recollection parsnips in this garden had perpetuated themselves. The tradition is, that Philip Call and his son were at work in a meadow. In the house were Mrs. Call the elder and her daughter-in-law, who at the time had an infant in her arms. Seeing the Indians coming, the young woman crept in behind the chimney, hushed her child, and was not discovered by them. Mrs. Call was killed, and the Indians departed. Mr. Webster's father bought the farm of Philip Call; and John Call, the preserved child, Mr. Webster knew in early life.

The dwellings on Elms Farm consist of the house with which were associated all his earlier and more precious recollections, also the one occupied by himself during his annual sojourn in the Granite State, and the one occupied by the tenant of the farm; while the barns and other outhouses number about a dozen, all painted white, and kept in the nicest possible order. A rail-road, connecting the Upper Connecticut River with Boston, crosses the farm in rather a picturesque manner, so that its proprietor could dine among the mountains and partake of his supper some three hours later in the capital of New England. It was in his house on this farm, with the tombs of his family before him at the end of a beautiful field, that the famous letter to *Hülsemann* was written. Directly in front of this house are a number of elm and maple trees, which were planted by Mr. Webster, and one of them, especially, was transplanted from the foot of a neighboring hill, where, when a boy, he once froze his feet while sliding in the snow.

Mr. Webster's reputation as a practical agriculturist was coextensive with his native state, and indeed with New England; and that it was justly so, the following figures, obtained from the tenant of Elms Farm, alone will prove. The yield of the farm during the year 1851 was estimated thus: of English hay, one hundred and forty tons, of potatoes, consisting of five varieties, two thousand bushels; of sheep, four hundred and fifty; and of cattle, one hundred. One yoke of oxen, when completely dressed, weighed twenty-nine hundred pounds, and were sold in the Boston market at seven dollars per hundred.

While upon his visit to Elms Farm in 1851, Mr. Webster's tenant had about twenty men in his employ making hay. On one occasion, when they were engaged in one field, the "Lord of the Manor" went forth to witness their operations, and having stood for some time in silence, the smell of the hay gave new life to the blood of his youth, and taking off his coat, and throwing it upon the ground, he demanded a fork and went to work, declaring that he could "pitch more hay in an hour than any man in the crowd." And he verily fulfilled his promise. He helped load the largest wagon no less than three times, and also performed the duties of wagon-boy in as scientific a manner, too, as if this had been the chief business of his life, instead of helping to manage the wheels of government, officiating as a diplomatist, or delighting a listening Senate with his eloquence.

The following story was related by Mr. Webster during a conversation the writer had with him about the early history of New Hampshire, while taking a morning walk along the Merrimack:

Among the many prisoners who were taken by the *Conewago* Indians during the old French war of 1756, in the immediate vicinity of Elms Farm, and sold to the French in Canada, was a man named Peter Bowen. When peace was declared, he obtained his liberty and returned to his family, who resided in Boscawen. In the year 1763, two Indians of the Conewago tribe, Sebat and his son, came from the borders of Canada upon a visit to the valley of the Merrimack, and happening to fall into the company of Bowen, spent the night with him for old acquaintance' sake, and, in the enthusiasm brought on by forest recollections, the party went through the performances of a drunken frolic. When the time came for the Indians to return, Bowen accompanied them a few miles on their way, when, as they were in the act of crossing a small stream running through Elms Farm, and now known as Indian Brook, the white man suddenly fell upon his red friends, shooting one and killing the other with the butt of his gun, and secreted their bodies in the top of a fallen tree.

Weeks passed on, and it was rumored far and near that Sebat and his son had been murdered, and that Bowen was the murderer. The inhabitants of the Merrimack valley were well acquainted with the characteristic code of the Indians, demanding blood for blood, and, in self-defense, thought it their duty to have Bowen arrested and punished. He was arrested, tried, found guilty, and condemned to be hung, and this intelligence was transmitted to the Conewago Indians.

During the imprisonment of Bowen, however, in the jail at Exeter (to which he had to be removed), a portion of the inhabitants became impressed with the idea that no white man ought to be hung for killing an Indian, whereupon a party of them, disguised as Mohawk Indians, broke the Exeter jail open and gave Bowen his freedom, and he lived in peace on his farm during the remainder of his days.

When Bowen died, he left his farm to an only son, who lived quietly upon it until he was seventy years of age, and the head of a large family. The story of his father's wickedness in murdering the Indians, though it occurred before his birth, had tinged with gloom even his happier days, and now the thought came to possess his mind that he must atone for the deed committed by his father. His friends remonstrated, but nothing could deter him from his purpose. He parted with his family; many tears were shed and lamentations uttered, but he entered upon his line of march for Canada, feeble and old, and gave himself up as a prisoner to the Conewago nation. The Indians were astonished at this instance of heroism, and, instead of taking blood for blood, they adopted him as a chief among their chiefs, and subsequently permitted him to return to the Merrimack valley, where he died in the midst of his children.

On one occasion, some years ago, when Mr. Webster was visited at Elms Farm by some two or three hundred of his New Hampshire friends, he addressed them, as was his wont, in a friendly and familiar way, giving an account, as it were, of his stewardship in the capacity of a statesman. He stood upon the porch of his own residence, and in full view of the family burying-ground, and after reaffirming the opinions he had long entertained upon the prominent questions of the day, he concluded his remarks by saying, "And before changing these opinions, fellow-citizens, you will be called upon to convey my body to yonder grave-yard." He uttered the sentiment while laboring under the deepest emotion, and its effect upon his audience was to melt them to tears.

The name of Mr. Webster's tenant on Elms Farm is John Taylor. He was transported thither about twenty years ago from the region of Marshfield, and in several particulars he is a great man. His height is *nearly* six feet and five inches; he has a heart bigger than his body, and is really a superb specimen of American yeomanry. But his reigning peculiarity was his attachment to his landlord. When the latter was temporarily ill during the summer of 1851, John Taylor watched by his bedside night after night without closing his eyes, performing all the delicate duties of a nurse with the gentleness of a woman. "If I saw a bullet coming to his heart," said he to the writer, on one occasion, "I would jump in the way of it, and receive it myself;" and when told that this was very strong language, he added, "I know it is, but then I should be certain that my family would be provided for and made comfortable. From no man living could a greater number of personal anecdotes be obtained calculated to illustrate the more endearing attributes of Mr. Webster's heart; how he was with him, for example, when he gave an old man, a friend of his father's, money enough to buy a small farm; how he accompanied him to the summit of a hill, one summer evening, and heard him talk in the most affecting manner, as he sat musing upon the spot where he was born, while his eyes were constantly filling with tears; and how, on many occasions, he had descanted to him, in the most glowing language, on the pleasures of farming, contrasting them with the trials and perplexities of a public life. John Taylor is also a first-rate farmer, and has performed as great an amount of hard labor as any other man in the Union, and is deserving, in every particular, of the ardent friendship and unlimited confidence of his late landlord.

In some long talks that the writer had with John Taylor about Mr. Webster, much was said about his knowledge of farming; and by way of exhibiting this, the following familiar letters, selected from a large number of like character, were copied, and are now printed from the journals in which they originally appeared, before the request of the literary executors had been made known.

"Washington, March 13th, 1852.

"John Taylor,

"I am glad to hear from you again, and to learn that you are all well, and that your teams and tools are ready for spring's work, whenever the weather will allow you to begin. I sometimes read books on farming; and I remember that a very sensible old author advises farmers 'to plow naked and to sow naked.' By this he means that there is no use in beginning spring's work till the weather is warm, that a farmer may throw aside his winter clothes and roll up his sleeves. Yet he says we ought to begin as early in the year as possible. He wrote some very pretty verses on this subject, which, as far as I remember, run thus:

"'While yet the spring is young, while earth unbinds
The frozen bosom to the western winds;

While mountain snows dissolve against the sun,
And streams, yet new, from precipices run—
E'en in this early dawning of the year,
Produce the plow, and yoke the sturdy steer;
And goad him till he smoke beneath his toil,
And the bright share is buried in the soil.'

"John Taylor, when you read these lines, do you not see the snow melting, and the little streams beginning to run down the southern slopes of your Punch-brook pasture, and the new grass starting and growing in the trickling water, all green, bright, and beautiful? and do you not see your Durham oxen smoking from heat and perspiration as they draw along your great breaking-up plow, cutting and turning over the tough sward in your meadow in the great field? The name of this sensible author is Virgil; and he gives farmers much other advice, some of which you have been following all this winter without even knowing that he had given it.

"'But when cold weather, heavy snows, and rain,
The laboring farmer in his house restrain,
Let him forecast his work, with timely care,
Which else is huddled when the skies are fair;
Then let him mark the sheep, and whet the shining share,
Or hollow trees for boats, or number o'er
His sacks, or measure his increasing store;
Or sharpen stakes, and mend each rake and fork,
So to be ready, in good time, to work—
Visit his crowded barns at early morn,
Look to his granary, and shell his corn;
Give a good breakfast to his numerous kine,
His shivering poultry, and his fattening swine.'

"And Mr. Virgil says some other things, which you understand up at Franklin as well as ever he did:

"'In chilling winter, swains enjoy their store,
Forget their hardships, and recruit for more;
The farmer to full feasts invites his friends,
And what he got with pains, with pleasure spends;
Draws chairs around the fire, and tells, once more,
Stories which often have been told before;
Spreads a clean table with things good to eat,
And adds some moistening to his fruit and meat;
They praise his hospitality, and feel
They shall sleep better after such a meal.'

"John Taylor, by the time you have got through this, you will have read enough. The sum of all is, be ready for your spring's work as soon as the weather becomes warm enough, and then put your hand to the plow, and look not back. DANIEL WEBSTER."

"Washington, March 17th, 1852.

"JOHN TAYLOR,

"Go ahead. The heart of the winter is broke, and before the first day of April all your land may be plowed. Buy the oxen of Captain Marston, if you think the price fair. Pay for the hay. I send you a check for $160, for these two objects. Put the great oxen in a condition to be turned out and fattened. You have a good horse-team, and I think, in addition to this, four oxen and a pair of four-year-old steers will do your work. If you think so, then dispose of the Stevens oxen, or unyoke them, and send them to the pasture, for beef. I know not when I shall see you, but I hope before planting. If you need any thing, such as guano, for instance, write to Joseph Buck, Esq., Boston, and he will send it to you. Whatever ground you sow or plant, see that it is in good condition. We want no *pennyroyal crops.* 'A little farm well tilled,' is to a farmer the next best thing to 'a little wife well willed.' Cultivate your garden. Be sure to produce sufficient quantities of useful vegetables. A man may half support his family from a good garden. Take care to keep my mother's garden in good order, even if it cost you the wages of a man to take care of it. I have sent you many garden seeds. Distribute them among your neighbors. Send them to the stores in the village, that every body may have a part of them without cost. I am glad that you have chosen Mr. Pike representative. He is a true man; but there are in New Hampshire many persons who call themselves Whigs, who are no Whigs at all, and no better than disunionists. Any man who hesitates in granting and securing to every part of the country its just and constitutional rights, is an enemy to the whole country. John Taylor! if one of your boys should say that he honors his father and mother, and loves his brothers and sisters, but still insists that one of them shall be driven out of the family, what can you say of him but this, that there is no real family love in him? You and I are farmers; we never talk politics—our talk is of oxen; but remember this: that any man who attempts to excite one part of this country against another, is just as wicked as he would be who should attempt to get up a quarrel between John Taylor and his neighbor, old Mr. John Sanborn, or his other neighbor, Captain Burleigh. There are some animals that live best in the fire; and there are some men who delight in heat, smoke, combustion, and even general conflagration. They do not follow the things which make for peace. They enjoy only controversy, contention, and strife. Have no communion with such persons, either as neighbors or politicians. You have no more right to say that slavery ought not to exist in Virginia, than a Virginian has to say that slavery ought to exist in New Hampshire. This is a question left to every state to decide for itself; and if we mean to keep the states together, we must leave to every state this power of deciding for itself. I think I never wrote you a word before upon politics. I shall not do it again. I only say love your country, and your whole country; and when men attempt to persuade you to get into a quarrel with the laws of other states, tell them 'that you mean to mind your own business,' and advise them to mind theirs. John Taylor, you are a free man; you possess good principles; you have a large family to rear and provide for by your labor. Be thankful to the government which does not oppress you, which does not bear you down by excessive taxation, but which holds out to you and to yours the hope of all the blessings which liberty, industry, and security may give. John Taylor, thank God, morning and evening, that you were born in such a country. John Taylor! never write me another word upon politics. Give my kindest remembrance to your wife and children; and when you look from your eastern windows upon the graves of my family, remember that he who is the author of this letter must soon follow them to another world.

"DANIEL WEBSTER."

Mr. Webster was often heard to say that he never enjoyed himself to such perfection in any place whatsoever, as when spending a few weeks at midsummer upon his New Hampshire farm. The associations of his birth-place and boyhood seem to have had an iron grasp upon his affections, which even the important duties and high aspirations of the statesman could not cloy or render insipid. And when there, he visited, and was visited by, his sturdy and very worthy neighbors without any ceremony. Throughout the whole region was he spoken of as "*the squire*," and, while the nation and the world admired him for his intellect, his rustic friends loved him for the goodness of his heart. Many called upon him simply to shake him by the hand and inquire after his health; some came to consult him on topics connected with agriculture; and others, in the simplicity of their hearts, thought it perfectly proper to consult him in regard to their petty lawsuits; and he ever treated them, as a matter of course, with the utmost kindness, helping them out of their troubles "without money and without price." To those who have been in the habit of paying him retaining fees of five thousand dollars or more, such conduct on the part of Mr. Webster must indeed appear strange.

The last time Mr. Webster visited Elms Farm, which was in July last, the writer was his only companion. All along the rail-road, on our way from Boston to the mountains, groups and crowds of people were assembled to welcome him to his native state; but this had for so long a time been a consequence of his annual visits to Elms Farm, that he was therefore not taken by surprise. At Concord he heard the particulars of an accident which had happened to his man John Taylor, and when told that his life was in danger, he was sadly distressed, and manifested great impatience to reach home. On alighting from the cars and stepping upon his threshold, he only took time to cast one loving look at his noble rows of elms and broad fields just ready for the scythe, before he went to visit his tenant. Though he found his yeoman friend suffering from a dislocated shoulder, a dreadfully bruised breast, and a fearful gash in his thigh, some seven inches long, yet the doctor had declared him out of danger. With this news Mr. Webster was, of course, delighted. Before he left Boston he had heard of the accident, but no particulars; and as he did not apprehend any danger, his first thought was, "What shall I take John Taylor as a present?" which question he answered by bringing him a *basket of grapes* and a *fresh salmon*. The present was fit for a king, but John Taylor deserved it.

The accident alluded to was caused by an angry bull, who turned upon his keeper in a fit of causeless anger, and not only tossed him high into the air with his horns, but trampled him under his feet. It is a wonder the man was not killed. What saved him was the presence of mind which he manifested in seizing and holding on to a ring in the bull's nose. In spite of his wickedness, this animal deserves a passing notice in this connection, as he was a very great favorite with his owner. He was presented to Mr. Webster by his devoted friend, Roswell L. Colt, Esq., of New Jersey, and he is of what is called the *Hungarian breed.* He is a magnificent creature, quite young, weighs some two thousand pounds, of a beautiful mouse or slate color, and has a neck which measures more than six feet in circumference. John Taylor's account of the attack upon himself, and of other exploits of the bull, was very amusing; and when asked by Mr. Webster if he really thought the animal dangerous and ought to be chained, he replied, "Why, he is no more fit to go abroad than your friend Governor Kossuth himself." "Rather strong language this," replied Mr. Webster; "but when a man has been gored almost to death by a Hungarian bull, it is not strange that he should be severe upon the Hungarian governor."

A short time before we left Boston for Elms Farm, Mr. Webster directed the writer to go to a book-store and purchase some forty or fifty volumes of late English books for his use at the farm. He left the selection entirely to the purchaser, and he was, of course, much gratified to know that his judgment in this rather delicate commission was fully approved. The collection consisted of one or two odd dictionaries, works on natural history, books of travel, a little history, and several volumes of correspondence, but not a fragment on politics.

A number of reviews were also sent up by the booksellers, containing elaborate articles about himself, and the complete edition of his works. When he found him at leisure, the writer handed him these, but he would not look at them. The writer then told him that they were well written, and an offer was made to read some of them aloud, but he would not consent. The reasons that he gave for declining even to know what had been said were, that such things were not at all interesting to him;

that he had done his best through life, and that this consciousness was more comforting to him than the good opinions of those who knew him not; that he was getting to be an old man; that his candle of life was already in the socket; and that to one just entering life these things might be pleasant, but he was going off the stage, and had no taste for them; that if any body should misrepresent him in regard to facts, and he heard of it, he would set them right, but good opinions were of very little interest or real value to him.

And here the writer would record what he deems the effect, upon Mr. Webster, of the Baltimore Whig nomination for President. He was, indeed, by far the greatest of all the candidates brought forward by his party, and though his defeat must have caused some disappointment, he never for a single moment manifested any regret. He told the writer, on one occasion, that his friends had done all they could do for him, and he was satisfied; and then added, with a tremulous voice and tears in his eyes, "*Thank God, one thing is certain, they could not take away from me what I have done for my country!*" Of both the gentlemen who were nominated, the writer has heard him speak in terms of praise. Of General Scott, as a military man, he spoke in the highest terms, and said that Congress ought long ago to have made him a lieutenant general. General Pierce, he said, he had known from boyhood, and all his family, and in spite of some hard things which "Frank" (for so he designated him) had uttered against him some years ago, he was compelled to like him, to think him a good fellow, a smarter man than people thought him to be, and wished him all prosperity. He was undoubtedly far more cheerful and happy after the nomination than he had been immediately before. With the convention alluded to terminated all his anxieties, and it is certain that he had of late been more anxious about quietly and faithfully performing his duties, both private and public, and preparing for the future, than about any thing else connected with this world.

Many were the delightful rides which the writer had the happiness to enjoy with Mr. Webster along the Merrimack Valley, and around and over the picturesque hills of his native Salisbury ; and it is with unfeigned pleasure that the writer remembers the fact that he was with him when he took his last ride over his farm, and visited for the last time the place of his birth. It was after a night of showers and a most charming day, we went in an easy double carriage, and the writer held the reins. He was personally acquainted with almost every body we met, and not only did he stop and exchange a word of kindness with his old friends, but he also bade me pull up the horses whenever he met a party of little children going to school or gathering berries, so that he might lovingly inquire their names and ask after their parents. He was in fine spirits, and seemed to be delighted with the singing of the birds, which positively seemed anxious to manifest their gladness at his presence. But alas ! those sweet and much-loved sounds will never again greet his ear. He looked with a critical eye upon all the fields and gardens, and every bit of scenery that we saw, fit for a picture, he expatiated upon most eloquently.

We rode through a part of the village of Boscawen, and he pointed out the spot where he went to school in his fourteenth year, and where he subsequently first became acquainted with Grace Fletcher (his first wife), whom he mentioned at that time, and always mentioned, as the "mother of his children." To her he was married in the summer of 1807, and she died in the city of New York in 1827. The visit to the spot of his birth was pleasant but mournful. We drank a cup of water together out of the old well, and it was with subdued feelings that he walked over the sod where he sported in childhood, and talked in the most affectionate manner of the olden times. As the writer has elsewhere remarked, the house *in which he was born* is not now standing, and it is due to the writer to state that the only authentic view of that house with the neighboring elm and well is the one which the writer drew, while Mr. Webster was bending over his shoulder, and an engraving from which embellishes this volume. The engraving which was published in the six-volume edition of his works represents the property *adjoining* that of the real birth-place, and was engraved by mistake, or, at any rate, without Mr. Webster's sanction. The authentic drawing was given to the engraver, but he strangely thought proper to substitute the handsome but false picture for the homely but accurate one.

Another place that we visited was the Big Pasture, so called, which belonged to Mr. Webster, and where he was then keeping about one hundred head of splendid cattle. The pasture contained nearly four hundred acres, and from the highest point there is a fine prospect of the White

Mountains. To see Mr. Webster in his regular farming suit, and with his white slouched hat on his head and a stick in his hand, walking among his cattle, which were collected together for his inspection, was indeed an interesting and beautiful sight. A stranger would have taken him for a stalwart drover or butcher selling or purchasing stock; while in reality he was the master-mind of the world. The writer was also privileged to wet a line for trout, while Mr. Webster sat in his carriage and looked on, in Punch-brook, upon which are located both the birthplace and the Big Pasture, and which empties into the Merrimack at Elms Farm.

We also took a drive around Lake Como, which is a beautiful sheet of pure water, distant from the farm some three miles, about two miles long, and surrounded with a handsomely-cultivated country. The lake abounds in perch and pike; and, of course, Mr. Webster ever had a fish-house there, and a boat in which he was accustomed to enjoy, and permit his friends to enjoy, the pleasant recreation of angling. On the borders of this lake we halted before a nice country house, flanked by a noble farm, when Mr. Webster sent in for its master; and on his appearance, introduced him to the writer as his "*very worthy nephew.*" The person thus introduced was a tall, thin man, who looked as if nature had formed him of its toughest sinews, and browned him with the hues of the most substantial health. The nephew returned the civilities of his distinguished uncle in a plain, blunt manner, but with affection; and little did he believe that the mere fact of his being thus connected would elevate him, in many parts of the country, into a decided lion.

We also visited the junction of those two mountain streams which form the Merrimack. The scenery at this point is wild and romantic; and as the immediate banks of the main river as you descend are rank with vegetation, and all the interval lands highly cultivated, and the residences of the farmers all neat and comfortable, a ride of half a dozen miles down the river is indescribably beautiful; and when enjoyed with *such* a companion, who recognized an old friend in every tree and stone, the reader may well imagine that the pleasure was unalloyed. By the writer it can certainly never be forgotten.

MARSHFIELD.

The birth-place and mountain farm of Mr. Webster having already been described in this volume, the writer would now give an account of Marshfield, the *home*, pre-eminently, of the distinguished statesman. The place thus designated is in the town of Marshfield, county of Plymouth, and State of Massachusetts. It is more of a magnificent farm, with elegant appendages, than the mere elegant residence of a gentleman; a place, indeed, which, if in England, could hardly be described without frequent use of the word baronial. It lies some thirty miles from Boston, comprehends about two thousand acres of undulating and marshy land, and slopes down to the margin of the ocean. The original owners of the land, now combined into one estate, were Nathaniel Ray Thomas, a noted Loyalist, who was the hero of Trumbull's poem of M'Fingal, and the famous Winslow family, which has given to Massachusetts, as colony and state, a number of her early governors. It came into Mr. Webster's possession somewhere about twenty-five years ago, and is the domain where he chiefly gratified his taste for, and exhibited his knowledge of, the interesting science of agriculture. The great good that he here accomplished in that particular can hardly be estimated; but for all the pains and trouble which the place has cost him, the proprietor was amply rewarded by the fact that he was the owner of one of the very best farms in the whole country.

Like Elms Farm, Marshfield has also its tenant or superintendent, whose name is Porter Wright, and who, in all particulars, is amply qualified for his responsible position. From him we gathered the information that when Mr. Webster came to Marshfield the farm yielded only some fifteen tons of English hay, while the product in this particular, during the year 1851, amounted to nearly four hundred tons, in addition to two hundred tons of salt hay; also, of corn eight hundred bushels, potatoes one thousand bushels, oats five hundred bushels, turnips five hundred bushels, and beets four hundred bushels. In 1825, the inhabitants of Plymouth county knew nothing of kelp and sea-weed as articles that would enrich their lands; but Mr. Webster discovered their value, set the example of using them, profited thereby, and they are now considered so indispensable that some of the farmers in the country will team it a distance of thirty miles. Principally at his own expense, Mr. Webster laid out a road to the beach on which the kelp was thrown by the sea; and not a single ton of the article is known to have been drawn on land before he went to Marshfield. In October of last year, one hundred and fifty teams were employed after a storm in drawing this rich manure on to the estates adjoining Marshfield, exclusive of those engaged by Mr. Porter Wright. And some of Mr. Webster's neighbors allege that they could well afford to give him five tons of hay a year for having taught them the use of ocean manure. In olden times, too, it was but precious seldom that the traveler's eye fell upon any but a wood-colored house in the vicinity of Marshfield Farm, while now neatly-painted dwellings may be seen in every direction, and many of their occupants acknowledge that Mr. Webster not only helped them to make money by giving them employment, but also taught them how to make themselves comfortable. Some of them, indeed, go so far as to say, that if the town of Marshfield had made Mr. Webster a present of thirty thousand dollars, they would only have rendered an adequate return for his agricultural services. He not only taught them how to enrich their soils, but in stocking his own farm with the very best of blooded cattle, he also, with a liberal hand, scattered them upon the farms of his neighbors.

Indeed, the raising of fine cattle was Mr. Webster's agricultural hobby, and it was a rare treat to take a walk with him over his grazing fields, or through the spacious yards adjoining his overflowing barns, and to hear him descant upon the goodness and beauty of his Alderney cows, with their gazelle eyes, or the brilliant color of his Devon oxen, and contrasting their excellences with those which distinguish the breeds of Hertfordshire and Ayrshire. A better judge of cattle than he was not to be found any where; and though his stables were abundantly supplied with horses, for these he entertained no uncommon attachment; but then, again, for sheep and swine he had a partiality. Of the latter animal he once raised a single litter of twelve, which were all entirely white, and when killed averaged in weight no less than four hundred pounds. And those who have a passion for the oddities of the quadruped world, might, by taking a short walk into a particular field, have a sight of several South American lamas, which helped to give a romantic character to the farm. And when the reader comes to add to the foregoing three varieties of geese, ducks of all kinds, domesticated in this country, Guinea hens, peacocks, and Chinese poultry to an almost unlimited extent, he may well imagine that the living animals of Marshfield compose a "cattle show" of no common order.

The mind that had the good sense to enrich Marshfield Farm with so much of the useful and interesting also covered it with the results of the most refined taste. The flower-garden, for example, covers nearly an acre of ground, and contains the richest and most beautiful varieties of plants peculiar to the country. Of forest trees, too, there is a multitudinous array, of every size and every variety; and it has been estimated that at least one hundred thousand of them have grown to their present size from seeds planted by Mr. Webster's own hands; for, as he has often said, when he originally came to Marshfield, he was too poor a man to think of patronizing such establishments as nurseries, even if they had existed to any extent. Of fruit-trees there is also an extensive collection; and while one orchard contains some three hundred trees, that remind one of the Pilgrim fathers, so weather-beaten and worn in their attire are they, another, of a thousand trees, presents the appearance of an army of youthful warriors; and then the farm is so appropriately intersected with roads and avenues, gravelly walks and shady pathways, that every thing which the visitor notices seems to be in exactly the right place, and is so completely come-at-able that the idea of being fatigued never enters the mind; and how pre-eminently was this the case when the visitor was accompanied in his walks by the ruling spirit of that place as well as of the country itself. But the value and pictorial beauty of Marshfield are greatly enhanced by the existence, in the immediate vicinity of the mansion, of a trio of little lakes, all of them fed by springs of the purest water. The two smaller ones are the favorite haunts of the common geese and the duck tribes; but the larger one, which studs the landscape very charmingly, is the exclusive domain of a large flock of wild geese which Mr. Webster had domesticated. He informed the writer that his first attempts to tame these beautiful creatures were all unsuccessful, until the idea occurred to him that perhaps they might be made contented with their civilized abode, provided they could have awarded to them small sedgy islands, such as were found at their breeding-places in the far north, where they might make their nests and remain undisturbed by the fox and other prowling animals. The experiment was tried; and while the geese were rendered contented with their lot, the lake itself has been greatly improved in picturesque beauty by its wild yet artificial islands. Indeed, the rural scenery of Marshfield is all that could be desired by the painter or poet; but when they come to add thereto an immense expanse of marsh land, veined with silver streams, dotted with islands of unbroken forest, skirted with a far-reaching beach, and bounded by the blue ocean, they can not but be deeply impressed with the magnificence of its scenery.

It now becomes necessary to mention the buildings of Marshfield Farm. They number some two or three dozen, at the least calculation, embracing the mansion and adjoining out-houses, the residence of the chief tenant, the dairyman's cottage, the fisherman's house, the landlord's agricultural office, several large barns, the gardener's house, and a variety of subordinate buildings. But the chief attraction is the mansion itself; the main part of it was built in 1774, but it has been more than doubled in size since then, and now appears like a modern establishment. It stands upon the summit of a grassy lawn, is partly overshadowed by a stupendous elm, and is completely surrounded with a piazza. The ground floor alone contains no less than nine handsomely furnished rooms, all opening into each other, the largest and most westerly one being a Gothic library. Pictures, pieces of statuary, choice engravings, and curiosities of every description, are displayed in the greatest profusion, and the feminine taste every where manifested gives a peculiar interest to the whole establishment. Among the more prominent art attractions are portraits of Mr. Webster, by Stuart and Healey; one of Lord Ashburton, by Healey; one of Judge Story, by Harding; portraits of Fletcher Webster and wife; one of the late Edward Webster; a Roman girl, by Alexander; cattle pieces, by Fisher; marble busts of Mr. Webster himself and of Mr. Prescott, and a bust and very beautiful crayon drawing of "Julia," the late Mrs. Appleton. The last-mentioned portrait took a most powerful hold upon the writer's imagination from the moment he first beheld it; and this impression was greatly strengthened by discovering that the spirit of this departed daughter, and most lovely, gifted, and accomplished woman, seemed to pervade the entire dwelling, where she had been the joy of many hearts. To her was Mr. Webster indebted for his library, as it now appears, for it was built after her own design ; and a more delightful place, especially when Mr. Webster was present, seated in his arm-chair, and in a talkative mood, could not be easily imagined. Mr. Webster's entire collection of books has been valued at forty thousand dollars ; but his law library is in Boston ; his agricultural and natural history library in a small office building, situated in one corner of the Marshfield garden ; while the miscellaneous library is alone collected in the Gothic library hall. But the works here found are all of a standard and substantial character, as the following specimens will show ; for here are to be seen Audubon's Birds of America ; the Encyclopædia Britannica ; the best editions of Bacon, Washington, and Franklin ; all the dictionaries that were ever heard of ; every thing good in the way of history and poetry, together with an extensive sprinkling of the old divines. And so much for a general description of Marshfield.

Of the many choice relics which adorn the mansion at Marshfield, there is not one that Mr. Webster valued more highly, or descanted upon with more feeling and affection than a small profile, cut in black, and handsomely framed, which is thus described in his own writing :

"My excellent Mother."

"D. W."

The likeness is that of a highly intellectual person, and bears a striking resemblance to Mr. Webster.

Directly in front of the Marshfield mansion, in a sunny and pleasant locality, are two small elm-trees, which were planted by Mr. Webster to the memory of his children, Julia and Edward. The ceremony of their planting was as follows: Mr. Webster had been missing from his study for an hour or more, when he suddenly made his appearance before his son Fletcher with two small trees and a shovel in his hand, and summoned his attendance. He then walked to the spot already designated, and, having dug the holes, and planted the trees without any assistance, he handed the shovel to Fletcher, and remarked, in a subdued voice, as he turned away, "*My son, protect these trees after I am gone; let them ever remind you of Julia and Edward.*"

Those who knew Mr. Webster best say that he has been a changed man since the death of these children.

The oldest house now known to be standing on the soil of Massachusetts is said to be the one originally built and occupied by several generations of the Winslow family; and this stands upon a lot comprehended in Mr. Webster's farm. It is an aristocratic-looking place; and, though weather-beaten and worn, applications are frequently made to rent it, but the proprietor respects it for its antiquity and associations, and, with characteristic taste, ever preferred to have it remain in a kind of poetic solitude.

Among the choice relics which enrich the Marshfield library is the collection of thirteen silver medals which were voted to General Washington by the old Congress, and which, long after his death, were purchased by Mr. Webster of a branch of the Washington family. The reader will probably remember that these medals were offered to Congress with a view of having them deposited in the National Library, and that a committee, of which the Hon. Edward Everett was chairman, strongly recommended their purchase at almost any price. Strange as it may seem, a heavy debate arose out of this proposition. Just at this time, it so happened that Mrs. Webster was deliberating about the purchase of a Cashmere shawl, when Mr. Webster suggested that she should, for the time being, go without the shawl, and that the money thus saved should be invested in the Washington medals. Mrs. Webster most joyfully assented, and in a very quiet way the medals were transferred into his possession. In the mean time, the conclave of wise men in the forum were debating the propriety of paying a trifling tribute to the memory of Washington; and, after exhausting their learning, and about one week of their valuable time, they concluded to purchase the medals, and were dumbfounded to find them altogether beyond their reach.

It comes not within the province of the writer to describe these thirteen medals in detail; but, as he learned from Mr. Webster that the *reverse side* of the principal one was partially designed by Washington himself, the following description is submitted:

Occasion.—Evacuation of Boston by the British troops.

Device.—The head of General Washington in profile.

Legend.—Georgio Washington, supremo duci exercitum adsertori libertatis comitia Americana.

Reverse.—Troops advancing toward a town which is seen at a distance; troops marching to the river; ships in view; General Washington in front, and mounted, with his staff, whose attention he is directing to the embarking enemy.

Legend.—Hostibus primo Fugatis.

Exergue.—Bostonium recuperatum 17 Martii, 1776.

The fittest of all men which this country has produced was Daniel Webster to inherit these testimonials of honor awarded to George Washington, for, in regard to patriotism and true greatness, these men were like twin-brothers.

Chief, in regard to age at any rate, among Mr. Webster's retainers at Marshfield is his friend Seth Peterson, whom he once mentioned in a speech as the author of an argument he had been uttering on the price of labor, and whom he designated as "sometime farmer and sometime fisherman on the coast of Massachusetts." A stout, brawny, sensible, jovial man is this "Ancient Mariner of Marshfield," whose home, *par excellence*, is Mr. Webster's beautiful yacht *Lapwing*. The twain have been boon companions for about twenty-five years; and the bays, and inlets, and headlands of Massachusetts Bay were as familiar to them both as the best fishing-grounds are to one, and the fields of learning were to the other. And Seth Peterson is a good shot withal, and during the duck and snipe shooting season was ever the constant attendant of Mr. Webster, as also when he occasionally went forth into a belt of forest-land, stretching parallel with the sea-coast of Plymouth county, for the purpose of killing a deer, which feat was sometimes accomplished before a late breakfast hour. As Mr. Webster was an early riser, he had a standing order that when he was at Marshfield, Seth Peterson should have the very first interview with him, and, while this was obeyed as a duty and considered a compliment, it resulted in a systematic arrangement for the day's sporting. The grace with which Mr. Webster was in the habit of doing every thing was as conspicuous in a fishing expedition as at a dinner-party or a diplomatic interview. He had a decided eye for the picturesque in all things, but especially manifested it in his costume; and it was exceedingly pleasant to observe the kindness of heart which he invariably manifested, when, on returning to his fish-house from a morning excursion far out at sea, he proceeded to parcel out his cod-fish and mackerel or tautog to his rustic neighbors. But those who would be made fully acquainted with Mr. Webster's many amiable qualities and his skill as a fisherman must consult Seth Peterson.

And, by-the-way, those who are in doubt as to the existence of a great sea-serpent may be pleased to know that the testimony of both Mr. Webster and his Skipper is on the side of the affirmative of this question. They both allege that they once saw some living animal answering to the popular description of this creature; and Mr. Webster informed the writer that a drawing, taken of one caught in Plymouth Bay, was pronounced by the naturalists of Boston a miniature resemblance of an animal found on the coast of Norway, near the great whirlpool, and delineated by Pontoppidam in his history of Norway.

The writer was once enjoying a morning walk with Mr. Webster over his Marshfield grounds, when we were joined by a Boston gentleman who came to pay his respects to the statesman. Hardly had we proceeded a hundred yards before a flock of quails ran across the road, when the stranger worked himself into an intense excitement, and exclaimed, "Oh, if I only had a gun, I could easily kill the whole flock; have you not one in your house, sir?" Mr. Webster very calmly replied that he had a number of guns, but that no man whatsoever was ever permitted to kill a quail or any other bird, a rabbit or a squirrel, on any of his property. He then went on to comment upon the *slaughtering* propensities of the American people, remarking that in this country there was an almost universal passion for killing and eating every wild animal that chanced to cross the pathway of man; while in England and other portions of Europe these animals were kindly protected and valued for their companionship. "This is to me a great mystery," said he; "and, so far as my influence extends, the birds shall be protected;" and just at this moment one of the quails already mentioned mounted a little knoll, and poured forth a few of its sweet and peculiar notes, when he continued, "There! does not that gush of song do the heart a thousand-fold more good than could possibly be derived from the death of that beautiful bird!" The stranger thanked Mr. Webster for his reproof, and subsequently informed the writer that this little incident had made him love the man whom he had before only admired as a statesman.

The last time but one that Mr. Webster visited the spot

where he had decreed that his remains should repose, the writer was his only companion. The tomb is on the soil of Marshfield, and was prepared for himself and family at a cost of one thousand dollars. It occupies the summit of a commanding hill, overlooking the ocean and the site of the first church ever built in the town of Marshfield, and is inclosed with an iron paling. When the writer visited this sacred spot, in company with Mr. Webster, the only words that he uttered during the visit were uttered while pointing to the tomb and the green-sward, and were as follows:

"*This will be my home; and here three monuments will soon be erected; one for the mother of my children, one each for Julia and Edward, and there will be plenty of room in front for the little ones that must follow them.*"

The monuments alluded to above have been erected. They are simple columns, about four feet high, resting on granite bases, and capped with marble. The inscriptions are as follows:

"GRACE WEBSTER,
Wife of DANIEL WEBSTER:
Born January 16, 1781;
Died January 21st, 1828.
Blessed are the pure in heart, for they shall see God."

"JULIA WEBSTER,
Wife of
SAMUEL APPLETON APPLETON:
Born January 16, 1818;
Died April 18, 1848.
Let me go, for the day breaketh."

"Major Edward Webster:
Born July 28, 1820;
Died at San Angel, in Mexico,
In the military service of his country,
January 23d, 1848.
A dearly beloved son and brother."

At the back of the family burial-plot is the tomb, of rough-hewn, massive granite. The floor lies six feet below the natural level of the site, and the roof rises as far, but is covered with a luxuriant sod, forming a green mound. Nothing can be more simple than the whole appearance of this sepulchre. The only thing which would distinguish it as a place of unusual interest is, the small, plain marble slab over the door, on which are inscribed in bold characters the revered name of

DANIEL WEBSTER.

TRAITS OF PERSONAL CHARACTER.

Under the above heading, it is proposed to exhibit some of the phases of Mr. Webster's character, by a series of disconnected paragraphs, which were recorded, in a note-book kept for the purpose, as time and chance determined. And for his own sake, the writer would again remind the reader that he is not writing a systematic biography; and though this may be termed a "disjointed chat of his," it is hoped that the lessons and information attending his plain unvarnished facts may not be the less welcome to those who were unacquainted with Mr. Webster.

As he attained to his prominent position chiefly by means of his own exertions, it is reasonable to conclude that he was always a hard-working man. All who knew him, knew this to be a fact. Because he was a man of giant intellect, and had to do with the greater national questions of the day, it has been supposed that his business habits were not plain and practical. This is a great mistake, and the writer will endeavor to prove the contrary, by sketching his habits while attending to his official duties as Secretary of State.

He was usually among the first at his post of duty in the department, and among the last to leave. The first business he attended to was to read his mail, and this he accomplished in a short time, and after a peculiar manner.

The only letters that he read with attention were the official ones, and, where the questions they brought up did not require investigation, were generally disposed of immediately; all political letters were merely glanced at, and then filed away for future consideration; those of a private and personal character were also laid aside, to be attended to or answered early on the following morning, at his residence; while every thing of an anonymous character was simply opened, torn in two pieces, and committed to the basket of waste paper. The amount of business that he sometimes transacted during a single morning may be guessed at when it is mentioned that he not unfrequently kept two persons employed writing at his dictation at the same time; for, as he usually walked the floor on such occasions, he would give his chief clerk a sentence in one room to be incorporated in a diplomatic paper, and, marching to the room occupied by his private secretary, give him the skeleton, or perhaps the very language, of a private note or letter. In addition to all this, he made it his business to grant an audience to all who might call upon him, receiving dignitaries with dignity, and all friends, strangers, and *even* office-seekers, with kindness and cordiality; and, in this connection, it may be well to state that those who made *short* visits were generally the most successful in attaining their ends, especially if said ends were "*their country's*," or OFFICE.

As touching his deportment toward his subordinates in office, it was invariably of the most agreeable character. It was his law that every man should both know and do his duty; but he treated them all as if he knew them to be possessed of feelings as sensitive as his own. The consequence was that every man in his department was a warm personal friend.

It was ever his habit, on all proper occasions, to attend to the legitimate duties of his position, either as lawyer, as statesman, or diplomatist; but he had a rule of long standing, which prohibited the introduction, by his friends and neighbors, of all political topics when visiting him in his retirement. When at Elms Farm, they might talk to him about the scenery, the legends, the history, the crops, and the trout of the Merrimack Valley; and when at Marshfield, they might talk about the ocean and its finny tribes, of all the manifold pleasures of agriculture, of literature, and the arts; but they must, if they would please him, keep silent on all the topics, without exception, which make mad the politicians of the day. Though it has been his fortune to figure extensively in the political history of the country, it is firmly believed that his affections have ever been far removed from all such vanities. The necessities of his country and his ideas of duty alone made him a politician.

"What little I have accomplished," Mr. Webster once said, "has been done early in the morning." Like nearly all those men who occupy prominent positions before the world, he was always an early riser. If on either of his farms, he literally rose with the lark, and went forth to enjoy the quiet companionship of his cattle; and if in the city, especially in Washington, he was up before the sun, and among the first visitors to the market, where he not only attended to the necessary duty of supplying his table, but also enjoyed the conversation of the various rural characters whom he met there, and with whom it was his pleasure to be on intimate terms. As his habit of early rising and going to market was known, many citizens, who had not otherwise an opportunity of seeing him, embraced these morning occasions of meeting him.

The time intervening between his morning walk and the hour of breakfast was always devoted to business, to the writing of letters, marking out *patches* for foreign governments, or unraveling the knotty political questions of the day.

There are very few men in this or any other country who possess the faculty of winning and keeping personal friends to as great an extent as did Mr. Webster. So simple and unpretending was he in his manners, and so kind-hearted and affectionate, that those who were privileged to know him intimately had their admiration greatly increased, and learned to love him with a devoted affection. That office-seekers should have entertained an opinion adverse to the above is not surprising, for his most devoted friends would not have the hardihood to assert that he had an unconquerable affection for this class of amiable gentlemen. On the contrary, he undoubtedly disliked them, as would any other public man who had been bothered by them for nearly half a century. The truth is, he did not treat them oftentimes with the severity they deserved; and there are a far greater number of instances to be mentioned of his giving offices to poor men than of his turning the cold shoulder to those whose chief ambition was to cut a dash. He was beyond all question as much a man of feeling as a man of intellect, and the writer has yet to learn the name of the first man, woman, or child who ever knew Mr. Webster and did not love him.

For a great many years past, Mr. Webster had a regular law office in the city of Boston, and supplied with a valuable library of five or six thousand volumes, which was, however, for the most part, in the keeping of a law partner. In alluding to this fact on one occasion, he informed the writer that it was with the utmost difficulty that he could ever bring himself to attend to any legal business when sojourning at either of his country residences. "It not unfrequently happens," said he, "that people come to me just as I am about to leave Boston for Marshfield, with the request that I shall attend to their suits. I decline the business, and they insist upon my taking it in hand. I take their papers, put them in my *green bag*, and determine that I will attend to their cases when at Marshfield. When arrived at this place, my mind becomes so taken up with its manifold enjoyments that I forget all about the green bag, *unless there happens to come a rainy day*. In that event I sometimes look at the musty papers; but it is not unfrequently the case that the bag travels from Boston to the sea-shore, and thence to the mountains and back again, without ever being disturbed. The truth is, you can not mention the *fee* which I value half as much as I do a morning walk over my farm, the sight of a dozen yoke of my oxen furrowing one of my fields, or the breath of my cows, and the pure ocean air."

In view of his apparent carelessness of time and opportunities, with what astonishment do we all look upon the recorded efforts of his brain!

Mr. Webster once remarked to the writer that no man could become eminent in any profession, and especially in the law, without the hardest and most laborious study; and, whatever of genius may be awarded to him, it is certain that he is chiefly indebted to his own personal exertions for his late commanding position as an orator, a statesman, a jurist, and a man of letters. He was ever in the habit of performing all his duties, official and private, like a downright business man; indeed, the entire story of his life proves him to have been at all times a practical man. Twenty-five years ago, for example, he was acknowledged to be one of the most, if not *the* most efficient laborer in the useful and arduous toils of the Congressional committee-rooms, and of practical legislation; and the country was indebted to him for not a few of the important improvements in our laws. The most remarkable is probably the Crimes Act of 1825, which, in twenty-six sections, did so much for the criminal code of the country. The whole subject, when he approached it, was full of difficulties and deficiencies. The law in relation to it remained substantially on the foundation of the act of 1790; and that, though deserving praise as a first attempt to meet the wants of the country, was entirely unsuited to its condition, and deficient in many important particulars. Its defects were immense and manifold, but Mr. Webster's act, which, as a just tribute to his exertions, bears his name, cured all those defects, and alone gave him the title of a humane benefactor of mankind. It is said that no man at that time but Mr. Webster, who, in addition to his patient habits of labor in the committee-room, possessed the general confidence of the House, and had a persevering address and promptitude in answering objections, could have succeeded in so signal an undertaking.

No man in the country was more fond of out-door recreations than Mr. Webster. He had no taste or fondness for in-door amusements. He never played a game of chess, or checkers, or billiards, or ten-pins, in his life; and it is said that he was equally ignorant of cards, unless it was whist, a game which he would play with ladies and gentlemen on a winter evening for an hour or so. To out-door sports he has always been addicted, and to this manly taste he was unquestionably indebted for the robust constitution of his manhood. In his childhood and youth he was far from strong; indeed, he was supposed to possess a feeble constitution. There are letters in existence written from one friend to another, in which it was frequently stated that young Webster would be likely consigned to an early grave, for he appeared like one inclined to consumption.

Mr. Webster admired, above all things, to see the sun rise, especially from his chamber window at Marshfield. He appreciated the moral sublimity of the spectacle, and it ever seemed to fill his mind with mighty conceptions. On many occasions, at sunrise, both in the spring and autumn, has he stolen into the chamber occupied by the writer, which looked upon the sea, and, with only his dressing-gown on, has stood by his bedside and startled the writer out of a deep sleep, by a loud shout somewhat to this effect:

"Awake! sluggard, and look upon this glorious scene, for the sky and the ocean are enveloped in flames!"

On one occasion the writer was awakened in a similar manner at a very early hour, when, lo! Mr. Webster, who happened to be in a particularly playful mood, was seen going through the graceful motions of an angler, throwing a fly and striking a trout, and then, without speaking a word, disappeared. As a matter of course, that day was given to fishing.

Much has been said and written about Mr. Webster's extravagance and negligence in money matters. He was not, indeed, a worshiper of Mammon; or, if the world will have it so, he knew not the value of money. But what matter! He never defrauded a neighbor, and he scorned, above all others, the character of a miser. He made money with ease, and spent it without reflection. He had accounts with various banks, and men of all parties were always glad to accommodate him with loans, if he wanted them. He kept no record of his deposits, unless it were on slips of paper hidden in his pockets; these matters were generally left with his secretary. His notes were seldom or never regularly protested, and when they were, they caused him an immense deal of mental anxiety. When the writer has sometimes drawn a check for a couple of thousand dollars, he has not even looked at it, but packed it away in his pockets, like so much waste paper. During his long professional career, he earned money enough to make a dozen fortunes, but he spent it liberally, and gave it away to the poor by hundreds and thousands. Begging letters from women and unfortunate men were received by him almost daily, at certain periods, and one instance is remembered where, on six successive days, he sent remittances of fifty and one hundred dollars to people with whom he was entirely unacquainted. He was indeed careless, but strictly and religiously honest in all his money matters. He knew not how to be otherwise. The last fee which he ever received for a single legal argument was $11,000; and it is a disgrace to the chivalric city of New Orleans that his just demand, amounting to $25,000, for his efforts in the great Gaines case remained unpaid at the day of his death.

Mr. Webster was one of the most hospitable of men: it always seemed to do his heart good to entertain his friends, and he understood the science of hospitality to perfection. While at Marshfield, he always had one or two guests under his roof, and sometimes a dozen. He never consulted them about how they wished to spend the day, but made all the arrangements, and then sent them or took them where he pleased, knowing well that such orders as he might give would be gladly obeyed. If the party consisted of six, he would send two of them after trout, one to take care of the ladies, and perhaps take the three others upon a fishing excursion in his beautiful yacht, Captain Peterson. He often took along with him some of his grandchildren, evidently for his own pleasure as well as theirs. He usually dined at a late hour, say from four to six, and rarely appeared at the dinner-table except in full dress. He was very particular in regard to these customs of etiquette, and the writer will never forget the reprimand he received from Mr. Webster for coming to the table, when his excellency Mr. Crampton was present, in a frock-coat. There was a pleasure in the sting, however, for it proved the reprover to be a friend.

No man could be a more devoted lover of nature and natural history than Mr. Webster; and very few were more thoroughly versed in its scientific mysteries. There was more truth than fancy in the remark which he sometimes made, that the world would one of these days be favored with a work on the "*Natural History of Marshfield*," from the mouth, in part, of Seth Peterson, and *edited* by Daniel Webster. Notes for such a work have really been made for many years past, and it is to be hoped the idea was not abandoned. Mr. Webster was ever in the habit of cultivating the acquaintance of naturalists, and Audubon was one of his warm personal friends. He thought every thing of the great ornithologist, and frequently invited him to Marshfield. On one occasion, when Mr. Audubon was there, he was presented by Mr. Webster with a wagon-load of miscellaneous birds, which the latter had ordered to be killed by his hunters all along the coast, and among them was the identical *Canada Goose* which figures so beautifully in the "Birds of America." Mr. Webster has said that the delighted naturalist studied the attitude of that single goose for an entire day, and that he was three days in taking its portrait.

It is well known that Mr. Webster was quite original in all his "little ways," as well as his great ones; but in none has he been more so than in his habit of punishing his children. In this particular he acted contrary to the Bible, and *has spared the rod.* Whenever he wished to punish one of his boys for misconduct, he summoned him into his presence, and, taking both the hands of the offender in his own, and pressing them with all his strength, would simply look sternly into the boy's face for a few moments, and let him go without uttering a word. And according to Mr. Fletcher Webster, this happy combination of physical force and moral influence never failed to make him a better boy, for the eye of his father was sure to haunt him many a day thereafter; and no man could wonder at this result who has ever seen that eye flashing in the heat of debate.

About three months before the death of Mr. Webster, while he was at Marshfield, among other things which had been sent by his direction from his residence at Washington, was a late and very fine portrait of himself, by Healey. During the day after it was hung, he called his little grand-daughter (the eldest child of his beloved "Julia"), and, affectionately kissing her, pointed to the portrait and said, "That is yours." Early on the morning following, while in his library, he wrote and sealed a letter, and sent to the little girl who was in an adjoining room awaiting breakfast. The letter was a beautiful one, and contained a touching allusion to her "amiable and accomplished mother;" and he expressed the hope that she would value the picture when the original was gone, &c. It was evidently written with feelings of sadness in view of his declining health, and it seemed to be his desire to seal in writing the fact that the picture was hers, lest there might, in the event of his death, be some little jealousy of feeling among his grandchildren in appropriating a relic so valuable. A portrait of himself had once been promised by Mr. Webster to her mother.

On one occasion, when Mr. Webster was Secretary of State, in 1841, he came home from the department, and stepping into his front parlor, took down from a mantlepiece a very beautifully ornamented basket, hung it upon his arm and disappeared. In the course of half an hour he returned to the house and handed Mrs. Webster the said basket *full of eggs.* She was, of course, very much astonished at this development, on account of the inappropriate nature of the deed, and accordingly inquired the cause; when Mr. Webster replied, that he had been all the morning discussing with the diplomatic corps the affairs of some half dozen of the principal kingdoms of the world, and, as he was fond of seeing both ends meet, he only wished to realize how it would seem for him, a Secretary of State, to turn from such imposing business to the opposite extreme, of purchasing, within the same hour, a basket of newly-laid eggs.

One of the most distinguishing characteristics of Mr. Webster's deportment, when among his friends, was his playfulness. When at either of his country residences, he was always the first to leave his bed in the morning, and often, from that time until breakfast, he made extensive use of his lungs by shouting and singing, and generally concluded his discordant melodies with the remark, that if there was any one thing which he understood above all others, it was singing. He had a fondness, too, for spelling out in the most unheard-of manner the various familiar remarks which he had occasion to utter. The lowing of a cow or the cawing of a crow has sometimes started him, not only to imitate those creatures with his own voice, but nearly all the other animals that were ever heard of. He was also in the habit, when in a certain mood, of grotesquely employing the Greek, Latin, and French languages, with a sprinkling of Yankee and Western phrases, in familiar conversation; and he had an amusing way of conjugating certain proper names, and of describing the characters of unknown persons by the meaning of their names. He was, withal, one of the best story-tellers in the world, and every thing he related in that line had a good climax. To use the language of one of his Boston friends, "he could relate an anecdote with wonderful effect, and nothing was more easy than for him to 'set the table in a roar.' His fund of anecdote and of personal reminiscence was inexhaustible. No one could start a subject relating to history, and especially to American Congressional life, about which he could not relate some anecdote connected with some of the principal characters, which, when told, would throw additional light upon the narrative, and illustrate some prominent trait in the characters of the persons engaged in the transaction. This great gift he possessed in a degree unsurpassed. Mr. Webster's 'table-talk' was fully equal to any of his more elaborate efforts in the Senate. He could talk, to use a somewhat misnomeric expression, as well as he could speak. He had a keen sense of the ludicrous, and loved and appreciated nice touches of eccentric humor. We have many reminiscences of his story-telling, for, when at Washington, we often had the pleasure of dining at his table. On these occasions it was the purpose of those present to draw him out; and to do this, it was but necessary to start some topic in which he felt an interest. We shall never forget his account of his visit to Jefferson, at Monticello, his analysis of the character and intellectual attainments of Hamilton, who, he thought, bore a closer resemblance to the younger Pitt than any other man in English or American history, and his anecdotes of Chief-justice Marshall, and old Mr. Stockton, of New Jersey, and of his ride from Baltimore to Washington in a wagon, with a stout, burly fellow, who told him he was a robber."

The last incident alluded to is said to have occurred to Mr. Webster before rail-roads were built, as he was forced one night to make a journey by private conveyance from Baltimore to Washington. The man who drove the wagon was such an ill-looking fellow, and told so many stories of robberies and murders, that before they had gone far Mr. Webster was almost frightened out of his wits. At last the wagon stopped in the midst of a dense wood, when the man, turning suddenly round to his passenger, exclaimed fiercely, "Now, sir, tell me who you are!" Mr. Webster replied, in a faltering voice, and ready to spring from the vehicle, "I am Daniel Webster, member of Congress from Massachusetts!" "What!" rejoined the driver, grasping him warmly by the hand, "are you Webster? Thank God! thank God! You were such a deuced ugly chap, that I took you for some cut-throat or highwayman." This is the substance of the story, but the precise words used by Mr. Webster himself in repeating it are not remembered.

There is not an artist in the land who has a better eye for the picturesque in costume than Mr. Webster. When entertaining a party at dinner or holding a levee, he always *looked the gentleman* superbly; when out upon a fishing excursion, he could not be taken for any thing but an angler; and when on a shooting frolic, he was a genuine rustic Nimrod. And hereby hangs an incident. He was once tramping over the Marshfield meadows, shooting ducks with Seth Peterson, when he encountered a couple of Boston sporting snobs, who happened to be in trouble just then about crossing a bog. Not knowing Mr. Webster, and believing him to be strong enough to help them over the water, they begged to be conveyed to a dry point upon his back. The request was of course complied with, and after the cockneys had paid him a quarter of a dollar each for his trouble, they inquired if "Old Webster was at home," for as they had had poor luck in shooting, they would honor him with a call. Mr. Webster replied "that the gentleman alluded to was not at home just then, but would be so soon as *he* could walk to the house, and then added that *he* would be glad to see them at dinner." As may be presumed, the cockneys were never seen to cross the threshold of "old Webster."

The Historical Address delivered by Mr. Webster in New York in February last has been often pronounced one of his happiest efforts. It is certainly the most classical of all. The excitement to hear him was very great throughout the city, and though the tickets were not originally purchasable, there were instances in which a hundred dollars were paid for a single admission. Two hours before he was to appear before the most magnificent of audiences, Mr. Webster was telling stories at his dinner-table, as unconcernedly as if he was only intending to take his usual nap. On being questioned as to what he proposed to say, he remarked as follows:

"I am going to be excessively learned and classical, and shall talk much about the older citizens of Greece. When I make my appearance in Broadway to-morrow, people will accost me thus, 'Good-morning, Mr. Webster. Recently from Greece, I understand; how did you leave *Mr. Pericles* and *Mr. Aristophanes?*'"

Brilliancy of diction and warmth of color, as it were, in Mr. Webster's written and spoken words did involve a want of profundity. When you heard him, you pronounced him to be emphatically a man of feeling; when you read his speeches, you were not less struck with the faultless precision of the reasoning, the unerring accuracy of the deductions. His chief characteristic, if one quality predominated over the other, was his earnestness of purpose. When Senator Bell, on the memorable seventh of March, 1850, observed that it was high time the people of this country should know what the Constitution was: "Then, by the blessing of Heaven," replied Mr. Webster, "they shall learn this day, before the sun goes down, what I take it to be." There could be no doubt that he was, in the language of the old English republicans, "thorough"—he felt what he said, felt it deeply, and clothed it in words which his hearers could not help feeling. It is told of one of his bitterest opponents, that during a powerful appeal of Mr. Webster to the Senate, he affected to disparage him, and pretended to read a newspaper while the "Expounder" was poring forth words of fire; but the flushed cheek and trembling hand betrayed the device, and left little room for surprise when it was discovered that the newspaper was upside down.

On the day preceding the one on which it was expected that Mr. Webster would deliver the address of welcome to General La Fayette in Boston in 1825, he happened to be out in his fishing yacht. Fish were not abundant, and his companions were just about giving up in despair, when Mr. Webster hooked a very large cod, and just as it appeared at the top of the water, he exclaimed, in a loud and pompous voice, "Welcome! all hail! and thrice welcome, citizen of two hemispheres!"

Indeed, Mr. Webster's sport of angling has given him many opportunities for composition—his famous address on Bunker Hill having been mostly planned out on *Marshpee Brook;* and it is said that the following exclamation was first heard by a couple of huge trout, immediately on their being transferred to his fishing-basket, as it subsequently was heard at Bunker Hill by many thousands of his fellow-citizens: "Venerable men! you have come down to us from a former generation. Heaven has bounteously lengthened out your lives that you might behold this joyous day."

In this connection the following particulars are worth mentioning. While his mind was greatly occupied with the affairs of the nation in the spring of 1851, he was even then in the almost daily habit of wetting a line at the Little Falls of the Potomac. His only and constant companion on these occasions was the writer, for whom he was in the habit of calling at the early hour of four in the morning. He was always delighted to capture a few rock-fish or bass, but if we happened to catch nothing he was quite contented, for he enjoyed the fresh air and the exercise. As we always returned from the fishing-ground before the public offices were opened, he took pleasure in congratulating himself with the thought that he had not robbed the government of any of its demands upon his time.

Mr. Webster's attachment to the Bible has already been mentioned; indeed, he loved and he read that priceless volume as it ought to be loved and read; and he once told the writer that he could not remember the time when he was unable to read a chapter therein. He read it aloud to his family on every Sunday morning, and often delivered extempore sermons of great power and eloquence. He never made a journey without carrying a copy with him; and the writer would testify that he never listened to the Story of the Savior, or heard one of the Prophecies of Isaiah, when it sounded so superbly eloquent as when coming from his lips. Those admitted to the intimacy of his conversation alone can tell of the eloquent fervor with which he habitually spoke of the inspired writings; how much light he could throw on a difficult text; how much beauty lend to expressions that would escape all but the eye of genius; what new vigor he could give to the most earnest thought; and what elevation even to sublimity.

It would be impossible, as C. W. March has said, for any one to listen half an hour to one of his dissertations on the Scriptures, and not believe in their inspiration, or *his.* And yet, while his private conversations and public productions attest how deeply he was imbued with the spirit of the Scriptures, neither the one nor the other ever contained the slightest irreverent allusion to any passage in them, any thing in the way of illustration, analogy, or quotation, which would seem to question their sanctity. He was scrupulously delicate in this regard; and therein differed widely from most of his contemporaries in public life; as he read and admired the Bible for its eloquence, so did he venerate it for its sacredness.

And, in continuation of the foregoing, the writer can not refrain from quoting the following passage from the pen of one, though anonymous, who seems to have fully appreciated the correctness of Mr. Webster's religious views and tastes:

"It was our fortune," says he, "to pass several days at his home in Marshfield, some six or eight years ago, and well we remember one beautiful night, when the heavens seemed to be studded with countless myriads of stars, that, about nine o'clock in the evening, we walked out and stood beneath the beautiful weeping elm which raises its majestic form within a few paces of his dwelling, and looking up through the leafy branches, he appeared for several minutes to be wrapped in deep thought, and at length, as if the scene, so soft and beautiful, had suggested the lines, he quoted certain verses of the eighth Psalm, beginning with the words, 'When I consider thy heavens, the work of thy fingers, the moon and the stars, which thou hast ordained; what is man, that thou art mindful of him? and the son of man, that thou visitest him? For thou hast made him a little lower than the angels, and hast crowned him with glory and honor,' &c.

"The deep, low tone in which he repeated these inspired words, and the deep, rapt attention with which he gazed up through the branches of the elm, struck us with a feeling of greater awe and solemnity than we ever felt when, in a year or two later, we visited some of the most magnificent cathedrals of the old world, venerable with the ivy of centuries, and mellowed with the glories of a daily church service for a thousand years. He was thinking then of that far-distant world, wherein it is promised that the good of this life shall live forever and ever. We remained out beneath the tree for over an hour, and all the time he conversed about the Scriptures, which no man has studied with greater attention, and of which no man whom we ever saw knew so much, or appeared to understand or appreciate so well.

"He talked of the books of the Old Testament especially, and dwelt with unaffected pleasure upon Isaiah, the Psalms, and especially the Book of Job. The Book of Job, he said, taken as a mere work of literary genius, was one of the most wonderful productions of any age or of any language. As an epic poem, he deemed it far superior to either the Iliad or the Odyssey. The two last, he said, received much of their attraction from the mere narration of warlike deeds, and from the perilous escapes of the chief personage from death and slaughter; but the

Book of Job was a purely intellectual narrative. Its power was shown in the dialogues of the characters introduced. The story was simple in its construction, and there was little in it to excite the imagination or arouse the sympathy. It was purely an intellectual production, and depended upon the power of the dialogue, and not upon the interest of the story, to produce its effects. This was considering it merely as an intellectual work. He read it through very often, and always with renewed delight. In his judgment, it was the greatest epic ever written.

"We well remember his quotation of some of the verses in the thirty-eighth chapter: 'Then the Lord answered Job out of the whirlwind, and said, Who is this that darkeneth counsel by words without knowledge? Gird up now thy loins like a man; for I will demand of thee, and answer thou me. Where wast thou when I laid the foundations of the earth? Declare, if thou hast understanding,' &c. Mr. Webster was a fine reader, and his recitation of particular passages which he admired was never surpassed, and was capable of giving the most exquisite delight to those who could appreciate them."

In further illustration of the foregoing, the following, from the pen of Francis Hall, Esq., of the New York Commercial Advertiser, is deeply interesting:

Some years ago," says he, "we had the pleasure of spending several days in company with Mr. Webster, at the residence of a mutual friend, Harvey Ely, Esq., at Rochester. During that intercourse we had more than one opportunity of conversing on religious subjects, sometimes on doctrinal points, but more generally on the importance of the Holy Scriptures as containing the plan of man's salvation through the atonement of Christ. So far as our knowledge of the subject extends, Mr. Webster was as orthodox as any man we ever conversed with.

"On one occasion, when seated in the drawing-room with Mr. and Mrs. Ely, Mr. Webster laid his hand on a copy of the Scriptures, saying, with great emphasis, '*This is the Book!*' This led to a conversation on the importance of the Scriptures, and the too frequent neglect of the study of the Bible by gentlemen of the legal profession, their pursuits in life leading them to the almost exclusive study of works having reference to their profession. Mr. Webster said, 'I have read through the entire Bible many times. I now make a practice to go through it once a year. It is the book of all others for lawyers as well as for divines; and I pity the man that can not find in it a rich supply of thought, and of rules for his conduct. It fits man for life—it prepares him for death!'

"The conversation then turned upon sudden deaths; and Mr. Webster adverted to the then recent death of his brother, who expired suddenly at Concord, N. H. 'My brother,' he continued, 'knew the importance of Bible truths. The Bible led him to prayer, and prayer was his communion with God. On the day on which he died, he was engaged in an important cause in the court then in session. But this cause, important as it was, did not keep him from his duty to his God. He found time for prayer; for on the desk which he had just left was found a prayer written by him on that day, which, for fervent piety, a devotedness to his heavenly Master, and for expressions of humility, I think was never excelled.'

"Mr. Webster then mentioned the satisfaction he had derived from the preaching of certain clergymen, observing that 'men were so constituted that we could not all expect the same spiritual benefit under the ministry of the same clergyman.' He regretted that there was not more harmony of feeling among professors generally who believed in the great truths of our common Christianity. Difference of opinion, he admitted, was proper; but yet, with that difference, the main objects should be love to God—love to our fellow-creatures. In all Mr. Webster's conversations he maintained true catholicity of feeling."

A few months ago, when Professor Sanborn, of Dartmouth College (who is the husband of one of Mr. Webster's nieces), happened to be in Washington City, he wrote a private letter to a friend, which contained the following interesting passage: "A few evenings since, sitting by his own fireside, after a day of severe labor in the Supreme Court, Mr. Webster introduced the last Sabbath's sermon, and discoursed in animated and glowing eloquence for an hour on the great truths of the Gospel. I can not but regard the opinions of such a man in some sense as public property. This is my apology for attempting to recall some of those remarks which were uttered in the privacy of the domestic circle. Said Mr. Webster, 'Last Sabbath I listened to an able and learned discourse upon the evidences of Christianity. The arguments were drawn from prophecy, history, with internal evidence. They were stated with logical accuracy and force; but, as it seemed to me, the clergyman failed to draw from them the right conclusion. He came so near the truth that I was astonished that he missed it. In summing up his arguments, he said, the only alternative presented by these evidences is this: either Christianity is true, or it is a delusion produced by an excited imagination. Such is not the alternative,' said the critic, 'but it is this: the Gospel is either true history, or it is a consummate fraud; it is either a reality or an imposition. Christ was what he professed to be, or he was an impostor. There is no other alternative. His spotless life in his earnest enforcement of the truth—his suffering in its defense, forbid us to suppose that he was suffering an illusion of a heated brain. Every act of his pure and holy life shows that he was the author of truth, the advocate of truth, the earnest defender of truth, and the uncompromising sufferer for truth. Now, considering the purity of his doctrines, the simplicity of his life, and the sublimity of his death, is it possible that he would have died for an illusion? In all his preaching the Savior made no popular appeals. His discourses were all directed to the individual. Christ and his apostles sought to impress upon every man the conviction that he must stand or fall alone—he must live for himself and die for himself, and give up his account to the omniscient God, as though he were the only dependent creature in the universe. The Gospel leaves the individual sinner alone with himself and his God. To his own Master he stands or falls. He has nothing to hope from the aid and sympathy of associates. The deluded advocates of new doctrines do not so preach. Christ and his apostles, had they been deceivers, would not have so preached. If clergymen in our days would return to the simplicity of the

Gospel, and preach more to individuals and less to the crowd, there would not be so much complaint of the decline of true religion. Many of the ministers of the present day take their text from St. Paul, and preach from the newspapers. When they do so, I prefer to enjoy my own thoughts rather than to listen. I want my pastor to come to me in the spirit of the Gospel, saying, "You are mortal! your probation is brief; your work must be done speedily; you are immortal too. You are hastening to the bar of God; the Judge standeth before the door." When I am thus admonished, I have no disposition to muse or to sleep. These topics,' said Mr. Webster, 'have often occupied my thoughts, and if I had time I would write on them myself.'

"The above remarks are but a meagre and imperfect abstract from memory of one of the most eloquent sermons to which I ever listened."

One of the most peculiar traits of Mr. Webster's character was his memory with regard to men and names. There probably never lived a man who was personally acquainted with so many men, whether distinguished or obscure. He always seemed posted up with regard to what every body had said or done. By way of illustrating this fact, the following memorandums of answers to two questions, proposed by the writer during an evening conversation, are appended:

"The verses beginning '*You'd scarce expect one of my age*,' which are generally found in the school-books credited to Edward Everett, were written by *David Everett*. He was an educated man of considerable genius and talent, born, I think, in Massachusetts, and reared to the bar. If I mistake not, he studied law in New Hampshire, at Amherst, where he practiced his profession for many years, and held the office of County Solicitor. He was a pleasant speaker and an agreeable man. His politics were of the Democratic school, and I think he was at one time concerned in the editorship of one of the Boston journals. Several of his orations and addresses were printed. He was at the bar in New Hampshire when I lived in that state. Always differing in political matters, we were yet friends; and he was accustomed to speak of my earliest efforts at the bar with warm commendation.

"'No pent-up Utica contracts our pow'rs,
But the whole boundless continent is ours.'

"I have often been asked if I knew the origin of these lines, and especially have been so asked by citizens of Utica, in New York. This shows how the authorship of such small productions, agreeable though they may be, passes away and is forgotten. Fifty years ago or more, when the American theatre was far more respectable, in my opinion, than it is now, Addison's tragedy of Cato was got up by a company in Boston, and represented, I think, at the old Federal Street Theatre. A prologue on that occasion was written by *Robert Treat Paine*, Jun., Esq., and these lines are part of that prologue. Robert Treat Paine, then Robert Treat Paine, Jun., was the second son of Robert T. Paine, one of the signers of the Declaration of Independence. He was bred to the bar, but did not follow Blackstone's example in bidding farewell to his Muse and giving himself up to his profession. He had a good deal of the spirit of poetry in him, and wrote many things indicative of genius and spirit. Among others, the song of Adams and Liberty, which was very popular in New England in its time. Some of its verses were travestied; for instance, the following lines occur in the song:

"'Roll on, loved Connecticut; long hast thou ran,
Giving verdure to nature, and freedom to man.'

"A wag altered the lines thus:

"'Roll on, loved Connecticut; long hast thou ran,
Giving shad to Northampton, and freedom to man.'

"Mr. Paine was christened Thomas Paine, which name he bore to his manhood, and then had it changed for his father's name, because he did not like to bear the same as that of the author of the '*Age of Reason.*' He was an intimate friend of the late Major Russel, for many years the editor of the 'Boston Sentinel,' and often contributed to the columns of that valuable journal."

MISCELLANEOUS MEMORIALS.

Of all the coincidences associated with Mr. Webster, there is not one to be compared for interest and beauty with the following: When he delivered his argument on the Girard Will, in the Supreme Court of the United States, the excitement to hear him was truly intense. The array of women was unusually great during the entire three days that he spoke, so much so, indeed, that numbers of them, who could obtain no better position, sat upon the very floor, forgetful of all comfort. Although, when he entered the court-room, he intended only to deliver a dry, legal argument, yet when the effort was completed it was found to be a splendid sermon on the Christian ministry, as well as the religious instruction of the young; and among many others of equal merit was this passage: "When little children were brought into the presence of the Son of God, his disciples proposed to send them away; but he said, 'Suffer little children to come unto me.' Unto *me;* he did not send them first for lessons in morals to the schools of the Pharisees or to the unbelieving Sadducees, nor to read the precepts and lessons *phylacteried* on the garments of the Jewish priesthood; he said nothing of different creeds or clashing doctrines; but he opened at once to the youthful mind the everlasting fountain of living waters, the only source of eternal truth, 'Suffer little children to come *unto me.*' And that injunction is of perpetual obligation; it addresses itself to-day with the same earnestness and the same authority which attended its first utterance to the Christian world. It is of force every where, and at all times. It extends to the ends of the earth; it will reach to the end of time, always and every where sounding in the ears of men, with an emphasis which nothing can weaken, and with an authority which nothing can supersede, 'Suffer little children to come unto me.'"

The coincidence alluded to consisted in the fact that, during the very hour of the very day on which the above paragraph was uttered, one of Mr. Webster's own grandchildren, the child of his son Fletcher, died in its mother's arms, and was indeed translated to the bosom of its Savior.

The following well-authenticated fact was related to the writer by an eye-witness, and is only a specimen of many that might be mentioned tending to illustrate the character of Mr. Webster's heart. Somewhere about the year 1826, a certain gentleman residing in Boston was thrown into almost inextricable difficulties by the failure of a house for which he had become responsible to a large amount. He needed legal advice, and being disheartened, he desired the author of this anecdote to go with him and relate his condition to Mr. Webster. The lawyer heard the story entirely through, advised his client what to do, and to do it immediately, and requested him to call again in a few days. After the gentlemen had left Mr. Webster's office, he came hurriedly to the door, called upon the gentlemen to stop a moment, and having approached them with his pocket-book in hand, he thus addressed his client: "It seems to me, my good sir, if I understood your case rightly, you are entirely naked; is it so?"

The client replied that he was indeed penniless, and then, of course, expected a demand for a retaining fee. Instead of that demand, however, Mr. Webster kindly remarked, as he handed the client a bill for *five hundred dollars*,

"Well, there, take that; it is all I have by me now. I wish it was more; and if you are ever able, you must pay it back again."

The client was overcome, and it may be well imagined that he has ever since been a "Webster man." Surely, a man who could command the admiration of the world by the efforts of his gigantic intellect, and also possessed the above self-sacrificing habit of making friends, must indeed have been a great and a good man.

Those upon whom will hereafter devolve the duty of writing, in detail, the life of Mr. Webster, will find a mine of intellectual wealth in his correspondence. The total number of letters that he has written is unusually great, even for a man of distinction, and though many of them are necessarily brief, a large proportion of them contain original opinions of peculiar value and interest. Since they have been addressed to persons in every sphere of life, from the lords and ladies of England, and the schol ars, farmers, and merchants of our own country, to those in the humble walks of life in every state of the Union, their "subject themes" are of course manifold; but it will be found that they are all distinguished either for wisdom, wit, learning, beauty, or affection. Indeed, in the opinion of the writer, a more delightful book could not be imagined than that would be, composed of a collection of Mr. Webster's letters. And in this place it may do no harm to mention, that there are in existence several volumes of manuscript notes which were recorded by two ladies who were members of his household during his visit to England, and which are almost exclusively devoted to his observations and opinions, as casually expressed in a familiar manner.

A number of highly interesting letters and autographic keepsakes were presented to the writer at various times by Mr. Webster, and though he cherished the belief that these were his own property, a different opinion has been expressed, and he submits without a murmur.

The following letter was written by Mr. Webster at five o'clock in the morning, and in the month of April, 1847, while upon a visit to Richmond, Virginia. It was addressed to Mrs. J. W. Paige, a lady connected with his family residing in Boston:

"Whether it be a favor or an annoyance, you owe this letter to my habits of early rising. From the hour marked at the top of the page, you will naturally conclude that my companions are not now engaging my attention, as we have not calculated on being early travelers to-day.

"This city has a 'pleasant seat.' It is high; the James River runs below it, and when I went out an hour ago, nothing was heard but the roar of the falls. The air is tranquil and its temperature mild. It is *morning*, and a *morning* sweet, and fresh, and delightful. Every body knows the morning in its metaphorical sense, applied to so many objects and on so many occasions. The health, strength, and beauty of early years leads us to call that period the 'morning of life.' Of a lovely young woman we say, she 'is bright as the morning,' and no one doubts why Lucifer is called 'son of the morning.'

"But the morning itself few people, inhabitants of cities, know any thing about. Among all our good people, not one in a thousand sees the sun rise once a year. They know nothing of the morning. Their idea of it is, that it is that part of the day which comes along after a cup of coffee and a beef-steak, or a piece of toast. With them morning is not a new issuing of light, a new bursting forth of the sun, a new waking up of all that has life, from a sort of temporary death, to behold again the works of God, the heavens and the earth; it is only a part of the domestic day belonging to breakfast, to reading the newspapers, answering notes, sending the children to school, and giving orders for dinner. The first faint streak of light, the earliest *purpling* of the east, which the lark springs up to greet, and the deeper and deeper coloring into orange and red, till at length the 'glorious sun is seen, regent of day' —this they never enjoy, for they never see it.

"Beautiful descriptions of the morning abound in all languages, but they are the strongest, perhaps, in those of the East, where the sun is often an object of worship.

"King David speaks of taking to himself the 'wings of the morning.' This is highly poetical and beautiful. The wings of the morning are the beams of the rising sun. Rays of light are wings. It is that the sun of righteousness shall arise 'with healing in his wings.' A rising sun which shall scatter life, and *health*, and joy throughout the universe.

"Milton has fine descriptions of morning, but not so many as Shakspeare, from whose writings pages of the most beautiful imagery, all founded on the glory of morning, might be filled.

"I never thought that Adam had much the advantage of us, from having seen the world while it was new.

"The manifestations of the power of God, like his mercies, are 'new every *morning*,' and fresh every moment.

"We see as fine rising of the sun as even Adam saw, and its rising are as much a miracle now as they were in his day, and I think a good deal more, because it is now a part of the miracle that for thousands and thousands of years he has come to his appointed time without the variation of a millionth part of a second. Adam could not tell how this might be.

"I know the morning—I am acquainted with it, and I love it. I love it, fresh and sweet as it is—a daily new creation, breaking forth and calling all that have life, and breath, and being to new adoration, new enjoyments, and new gratitude."

The following extract from a letter will be read with interest. It was written from Franklin, New Hampshire, on the 3d of May, 1846:

"Sunday, 1 o'clock.

"MY DEAR SIR,

* * * * * *

"I have made satisfactory arrangements respecting the house; the best of which is, that I find I can leave it where it is (that is, the main house), and yet be comfortable, notwithstanding the rail-road. This saves a great deal of expense.

* * * * * *

"This house faces due north. Its front windows look toward the River Merrimack. But then the river soon turns to the south, so that the eastern windows look toward the river also. But the river has so deepened its channel in this stretch of it, in the last fifty years, that we can not see its water without approaching it, or going back to the higher lands behind us. The history of this change is of considerable importance in the philosophy of streams. I have observed it practically, and know something of the theory of the phenomenon, but I doubt whether the world will ever be benefited either by my learning or my observation in this respect. Looking out at the east windows at this moment (2 P.M.), with a beautiful sun just breaking out, my eye sweeps a rich and level field of 100 acres. At the end of it, a third of a mile off, I see plain marble grave-stones, designating the places where repose my father, my mother, my brother Joseph, and my sisters Mehetabel, Abigail, and Sarah, good and Scripture names inherited from their Puritan ancestors.

"My father, Ebenezer Webster, born at Kingston, in the lower part of the state, in 1739, the handsomest man I ever saw, except my brother Ezekiel, who appeared to me—and so does he now seem to me—the very finest human form that ever I laid eyes on. I saw him in his coffin—a white forehead, a tinged cheek, a complexion as clear as heavenly light! But where am I straying? The grave has closed upon him, as it has on all my brothers and sisters. We shall soon be all together. But this is melancholy, and I leave it. Dear, dear kindred blood, how I love you all!

"This fair field is before me. I could see a lamb on any part of it. I have plowed it, and raked it, and hoed it; but I never mowed it. Somehow, I could never learn to hang a scythe. I had not wit enough. My brother Joe used to say that my father sent me to college in order to make me equal to the rest of the children!

"Of a hot day in July—it must have been in one of the last years of Washington's administration—I was making hay, with my father, just where I now see a remaining elm-tree. About the middle of the afternoon, the Honorable Abiel Foster, M.C., who lived in Canterbury, six miles off, called at the house, and came into the field to see my father. He was a worthy man, college-learned, and had been a minister, but was not a person of any considerable natural power. My father was his friend and supporter. He talked a while in the field, and went on his way. When he was gone, my father called me to him, and we sat down beneath the elm, on a hay-cock. He said, 'My son, that is a worthy man. He is a member of Congress. He goes to Philadelphia, and gets six dollars a day, while I toil here. It is because he had an education, which I never had. If I had had his early education, I should have been in Philadelphia in his place. I came near it as it was. But I missed it, and now I must work here.' 'My dear father,' said I, 'you shall not work. Brother and I will work for you, and wear our hands out, and you shall rest.' And I remember to have cried; and I cry now at the recollection. 'My child,' said he, 'it is of no importance to me; I now live but for my children. I could not give your elder brother the advantages of knowledge, but I can do something for you. Exert yourself; improve your opportunities; *learn, learn;* and, when I am gone, you will not need to go through the hardships which I have undergone, and which have made me an old man before my time.'

"The next May he took me to Exeter, to the Phillips Exeter Academy, placed me under the tuition of its excellent preceptor, Dr. Benjamin Abbott, still living, and from that time * * * *

"My father died in April, 1806. I neither left him nor forsook him. My opening an office at Boscawen was that I might be near him. I closed his eyes in this very house. He died at sixty-seven years of age, after a life of exertion, toil, and exposure; a private soldier, an officer, a legislator, a judge, every thing that a man could be to whom learning never had disclosed her 'ample page.' My first speech at the bar was made when he was on the bench. He never heard me a second time. He had in him what I collect to have been the character of some of the old Puritans. He was deeply religious, but not sour. On the contrary, good-humored, facetious; sharing, even in his age, with a contagious laugh; teeth all as white as alabaster; gentle, soft, playful; and yet having a heart in him that he seemed to have borrowed from a lion. He could frown — a frown it was — but cheerfulness, good-humor, and smiles composed his most usual aspect.

"Ever truly yours, &c.,

"DANL. WEBSTER."

It has elsewhere been mentioned that Mr. Webster was fond of the sea; a sail in his yacht, on a pleasant day, always seemed to afford him unalloyed delight. In speaking of its roar on one occasion, after a storm, he stated that this was called the *rote* or *rut* of the sea; that both words were correct, since they were from the one Latin root—*rota*. The *ruts* in the road, he said, were the effect of rolling wheels, while rotation meant repetition as well as succession. To learn a thing by *rote* was to fix it in the mind by repeated readings. The rote or rut of the sea, therefore, only meant the noise produced by the action of the surf breaking on the shore. An expression which was often used by Seth Peterson, "*the cry of the sea*," he thought very expressive, for it signified the deep, hollow groaning and wailing of the ocean, uttered as if in anger, or smarting under the lashing of the winds.

The following are the original notes of Mr. Webster's

speech in the Senate, on the 7th of March, 1850, and given by him to Hon. Edward Curtis the next day.

Introduction, &c.

Stirring times, winds let loose, &c. I speak for union —and quiet.

1. History of events which have brought on this state of things.

2. Slavery—how regarded now. North and South—Absolutists. Impatient waiters.

3. How regarded in 1789.

4. What has changed the view?

Religion, at the North—Cotton, at the South.

5. Acquisitions.

Cession by Georgia, 1802—Louisiana, 1803—Florida, 1819.

6. *Finally, Texas*, 1845.

This sealed the whole matter. Read Resolution.

MY GENERAL PROPOSITION.

7. *Who brought in Texas?*

"Northern Democracy." Votes in the two Houses. Mr. Dix—Mr. Niles.

8. Review my own speeches.

9. As to California and New Mexico, *the law of Nature.*

10. Then what is the value of the Wilmot Proviso? &c.

Polk.

11. Now the aggressions complained of South and North.

Secession. Conclusion.

12. Two ideas.

13. Conclusion.

The following will be read with peculiar pleasure as a specimen of Mr. Webster's poetry:

"THE MEMORY OF THE HEART.

"If stores of dry and learned lore we gain,
We keep them in the memory of the brain;
Names, things, and facts—whatever we knowledge call,
There is the common ledger for them all;
And images on this cold surface traced
Make slight impressions, and are soon effaced.

"But we've a page more glowing and more bright,
On which our friendship and our love to write;
That these may never from the soul depart,
We trust them to *the memory of the heart.*
There is no dimming—no effacement here;
Each new pulsation keeps the record clear;
Warm, golden letters, all the tablet fill,
Nor lose their lustre till the heart stands still.

"London, November 19th, 1839."

The following is a memorandum of Mr. Webster's conversation, touching one of his first schoolmasters:

"William Hoyt was for many years teacher of our county school in Salisbury; I do not call it village school, because there was at that time no village, and boys came to school in the winter, the only season in which schools were usually open, from distances of several miles, wading through the snow, or running upon its crust, with their curly hair often whitened with frost from their own breaths. I knew William Hoyt well, and every truant knew him. He was an austere man, but a good teacher of children. He had been a printer in Newburyport, wrote a very fair and excellent hand, was a good reader, and could teach boys, and did teach boys that which so few masters can or will do, to read well themselves. Beyond this, and perhaps a very slight knowledge of grammar, his attainments did not extend. He had brought with him into the town a little property which he took very good care of. He rather loved money, of all the cases of nouns preferring the possessive; he also kept a little shop for the sale of various commodities in the house, exactly over the way from this. I do not know how old I was, but I remember having gone into his shop one day and bought a small cotton pocket handkerchief, with the Constitution of the United States printed on its two sides; from this I first learned either that there was a Constitution, or that there were United States. I remember to have read it, and have known more or less of it ever since. William Hoyt and his wife lie buried in the grave-yard under our eye, on my farm, near the graves of my own family. He left no children. I suppose that this little handkerchief was purchased about the time that I was eight years old, as I remember listening to the conversation of my father and Mr. Thompson upon political events which happened in the year 1790."

Mr. Webster's father was a soldier in the old French war (so called), and, as already mentioned, also acquitted himself with honor as a captain under General John Stark, at the battle of Bennington. On the battle-field, as well as in the walks of civil life, they were fast friends; and the elder Webster used to say that General Stark always thought and talked a great deal more about his exploits as a trapper of beaver, and a hunter, and fighter of the red man and Frenchman, in his earlier life, than he did of his Revolutionary deeds. But Mr. Webster related the following characteristic anecdotes to the writer: He was about twenty-seven years of age, and professional business had called him to the then village, now known as the flourishing city of Manchester, where the famous general resided. The young lawyer called upon the hero for the purpose of paying his respects, and found him surrounded with friends, who, with him, were hard at work drinking flip. The parties were introduced, and the moment General Stark heard the name of Webster, he exclaimed in a loud voice, "Why, Dan Webster, you're as black as your father; and he was so black that I could never tell when his face was covered with powder, for he was one of those chaps always in the thickest of the fight."

It was while hunting in the immediate vicinity of Elms Farm that General Stark had been captured by the Indians and taken to Canada, where he was sold for a specific sum of money; and it is a common saying in that region, that whenever he heard his neighbors talking about how much any of them were worth, he invariably mentioned the fact that his own value had been positively ascertained, for the Indians had once sold him to the French for £40, and that a man was *worth about* what he would fetch.

Among the subordinates of the State Department at the present time (1852) is a very worthy colored man named Charles Brown, who has been in Mr. Webster's employment for about thirty years. Indeed, Mr. Webster has never been in Washington for any length of time, since he first entered Congress, without having by his side this faithful servant. A few years ago it came to Mr. Webster's knowledge that this servant had purchased a lot of ground and built him a comfortable house, whereupon he was questioned by Mr. Webster as to his unexpected success.

"Where did you get the money to purchase so fine a house?" asked he.

"I am glad to say, sir, that it all came out of your pocket," replied the man; "it is the money which you have given me on holidays and other occasions."

From this it would appear that his occasional free gifts were sufficient, in one instance, to make a man comfortable for life.

On one occasion, when Mr. Webster had consulted his physician (and a man of eminence too), and could not obtain an answer to a scientific inquiry, he made this remark:

"Why, doctor, there is no such thing as science, no mathematical science, in your profession or mine. Now I tell you to remember one thing: in every place and at all times, bear it as your motto—*Nobody knows any thing*."

Another motto, which he claimed to have made his own on commencing life, was this:

"*Since I know nothing and have nothing, I must learn and earn.*"

A Quaker gentleman of Nantucket once called upon

Mr. Webster, at his office in Boston, for the purpose of securing his services in a suit which was about to be tried on the island, and wound up his appeal by demanding his terms.

"I will attend to your case for one thousand dollars," replied Mr. Webster.

The client demurred, but finding that the lawyer would not visit Nantucket for a less amount than the one specified, he promised to pay the proposed fee, provided Mr. Webster would agree "to attend to any other matters that he might present during the sitting of the court," to which Mr. Webster consented.

The appointed time arrived, and Mr. Webster was at his post. The leading case of his client was brought forward, argued, and decided in his favor. Another case was taken up, and the Quaker assigned it to the care of Mr. Webster, when it was satisfactorily disposed of; another still, and with the same result; and still another, and another, until Mr. Webster became impatient and demanded an explanation; whereupon the client remarked:

"I hired thee to attend to all the business of the court, and thou hast done it handsomely: so here is thy money, one thousand dollars."

The concerns of his farm always engrossed a very large share of Mr. Webster's attention, and a talented contemporary justly remarks that he loved its labors, and the genial communion with nature which its associations so much favored. It was there that the magnanimous kindliness and tenderness of heart, which formed so large a portion of his character, made itself seen and felt by all who came within his influence. He was always happy when he could escape from the worrying cares of professional or of public life to the retired and homely pursuits of his Marshfield Farm. The most genial humor pervaded all he did and said while thus engaged. Of this, also, we happen to have a happy instance in a business note which he wrote to *Charles A. Stetson, Esq.*, of the Astor House, some three years ago, during his temporary stay at Marshfield:

"Marshfield, Sunday, Sept. 5th,. 1849.

"My dear Sir,

"The best pair of working oxen on my farm shall set out for your place on Monday. They are seven years old, large, handsome, perfectly well broke, and, for common cart-work on a farm, are a team of themselves.

"I shall send, also, a likely pair of three-year-old steers, which have been somewhat used to the yoke, but are not yet quite so well trained and drilled as a couple of dining-room waiters at the Astor House. If you wish any change in this arrangement, please address a line to me, or, in my absence, to 'Mr. Porter Wright,' as I may go *somewhere* to try to mitigate my horrid catarrh. If we do not hear to the contrary, the aforesaid oxen and steers will be among the Lynn people next Tuesday morning, where they may tremble for their skins.

"I hear nothing of the Alderney, but should be quite glad to know that she was soon to join a very small party of her own relatives here, viz., one male and one female.

"I am grieved to have not seen you here, and hope you

will be the very next visitor, after the President, if he should come, and an early one if he should not.

"I hope to leave off *sneezing* in about a fortnight.

"Yours very truly, always,

"DANL. WEBSTER."

This little note, so unimportant in itself, gives a pleasant glimpse into the spirit which brooded around the daily life of this great man, during his intervals of leisure and relaxation from the harassing anxieties of official place.

As an appendix to the foregoing note, it ought to be stated that Mr. Stetson is owner of the celebrated farm in Lynn so highly improved by the late Henry Coleman. The allusion to the Astor House waiters reminds the writer, too, that when he happened to be at the Astor House, soon after Mr. Webster's death, the servants, knowing the writer, and feeling deeply the national bereavement, flocked around him in crowds, and asked many minute questions about the closing hours of their great friend. Unfortunately, no satisfactory replies could then be given, for, owing to circumstances over which he had no control, the writer could not be present at the closing scene. Since the erection of the Astor House, Mr. Webster never had any other stopping-place while in New York.

When the remains of Major Edward Webster were brought home from Mexico, his sorrow-stricken father was sensibly affected by the alacrity with which the "citizen soldiery" of Boston paraded to pay martial honors to the gallant volunteer. And carefully did he garner up every anecdote of his son's services from those who were associated with him in the formation of the Massachusetts Regiment and its campaign in Mexico. On one occasion the writer presented him with a sprig of laurel, with which a melancholy interest was associated. Just before embarking for Mexico, Major Webster paid a farewell visit to some estimable friends who reside on the banks of the Merrimack, in Newburyport, and in a stroll culled a laurel flower. "Do you intend to carry with you materials for a victor's wreath?" inquired the companion of his walk. "No," he replied; "but you may plant the slip, and I will endeavor to prove worthy of the wreath on my return." The slip took root, flourished, and is now a beautiful shrub; and as Mr. Webster heard its history, he gazed upon the sprig taken from it as though he wished that his son could also have been spared, and laid it away carefully among his treasured mementoes. Such relics were sacred in his eyes, and many an autographic or floral trifle did he hallow toward the close of his life, by presenting it to some friend with words never to be forgotten by the recipient.

Few men who have ever figured at all in the National Legislature have ever had as little to do with state governments as Mr. Webster; and it was in alluding to this fact that he once made the following remarks, while upon a visit to the city of Syracuse:

"It has so happened that all the public services which I have rendered in the world, in my day and generation, have been connected with the general government. I think I ought to make an exception. I was ten days a member of the Massachusetts Legislature (laughter), and I turned my thoughts to the search of some good object in which I could be useful in that position; and after much reflection, I introduced a bill which, with the general consent of both Houses of the Massachusetts Legislature, passed into a law, and is now a law of the state, which enacts that no man in the state shall catch trout in any other manner than in the old way, with an ordinary hook and line. (Great laughter.) With that exception, I never was connected for an hour with any state government in my life. I never held office, high or low, under any state government. Perhaps that was my misfortune.

"At the age of thirty I was in New Hampshire practicing law, and had some clients. John Taylor Gilman, who for fourteen years was governor of the state, thought that, a young man as I was, I might be fit to be an Attorney General of the State of New Hampshire, and he nominated me to the Council; and the Council taking it into their deep consideration, and not happening to be of the same politics as the governor and myself, voted, three out of five, that I was not competent, and very likely they were right. (Laughter.) So you see, gentlemen, I never gained promotion in any state government."

The opinion that Mr. Webster entertained of his great compeer Mr. Clay, as here recorded, from a note taken at the time and when the latter was on his death-bed, gives us a new insight into his character. It was uttered at his own table, and is as follows:

"Mr. Clay is a great man, beyond all question a true patriot. He has done much for his country. He ought long ago to have been elected President. I think, however, he was never a man of books—a hard student, but he has displayed remarkable genius. I never could imagine him sitting comfortably in his library, and reading quietly out of the great books of the past. He has been too fond of the world to enjoy any thing like that. He has been too fond of excitement—he has lived upon it; he has been too fond of company, not enough alone; and has had few resources within himself. Now a man who can not, to some extent, depend upon himself for happiness, is to my mind one of the unfortunate. But Clay is a great man, and if he ever had animosities against me, I forgive him and forget them."

On one occasion, during a temporary illness, Mr. Webster received a visit, in his chamber at Marshfield, from an old friend who lived about thirty miles off. After a long talk about the olden times, the visitor touched upon the misfortunes and reverses he had experienced, and incidentally mentioned that he was anxious to obtain a good cow. Mr. Webster listened attentively, but said not a word. When the friend had risen to go, however, he summoned Porter Wright into his presence, and told him to show his friend the herd of cattle, and to deliver into his possession any one of the cows which he might fancy. The animal selected, and most gratefully accepted, was an Alderney, and worth about fifty dollars. And this is only one of many similar instances which might and will be recorded to the astonishing liberality of Mr. Webster.

The following neat and graceful speech was delivered before the Agricultural Convention, held in the City of Washington in June, 1852, on the occasion of the society's calling upon Mr. Webster to pay their respects.

"Mr. Wilder, and Gentlemen of the United States Agricultural Society,—I am happy to see you one and all. You do me no more than justice when you call me farmer of Marshfield. My father was a farmer, and I am a farmer. When a boy among my native hills of New Hampshire, no cock crowed so early that I did not hear him, and no boy ran with more avidity to do errands at the bidding of the workmen than I did. You are engaged in a noble enterprise. The prosperity and glory of the Union are based upon the achievements of agriculture.

"Gentlemen, I will say to you what I have never before said, that when, at forty-five years of age, I was called to Dartmouth College to pass my second graduation, I determined, in my humble manner, to speak of the agricultural resources of the country, and to recommend for their more full development organized action and the formation of agricultural societies; and if memory does not betray me, it was about the period of time that the first agricultural societies in this country were formed in old Berkshire and Philadelphia. (Loud cheers by delegates from Pennsylvania and Massachusetts.) And though I have never seen that unimportant production since that day, the partiality of some of my curious friends (bowing and laughing) may be gratified by exploring among the slumbering archives of Marshfield. When, some thirty years ago, I was at Marshfield, some of my kind neighbors made a call to inquire the state of a matter involving a bit of law, I told them, 'I have come to reside among you as a farmer, and here I talk neither politics nor law.'

"Gentlemen, I am naturally a farmer. I am most ardently attached to agricultural pursuits, and though I cultivate my lands with some little care, yet from the sterility of the soil, or from neglected husbandry on my part, in consequence of my public engagements, they afford no subsistence to myself and family. To you, farmers of the West and South, the soil of Marshfield may look barren and unfruitful. Sometimes the breezes of the broad Atlantic fan you; sometimes, indeed, unkindly suns smite you, but I love its quiet shades, and there I shall love to commune with you upon the ennobling pursuit in which we are so happily engaged.

"Gentlemen, I thank you for this visit, with which you have honored me. My interest and my sympathies are identified with yours. I shall remember you and this occasion which has called you together.

"I invoke for you an abundant harvest, and if we meet not again in time, I doubt not that hereafter we shall meet in a more genial clime, and under a kinder sun. Brother farmers, I bid you good-morning."

Mr. Webster became a communicant of the orthodox Church when in the early prime of his life, and the following simple but interesting incident has become a fireside tale in and about the town of Franklin. The only person who occupied the pew with him at the time was a very poor and a very old woman, and during the singing of the hymn which concluded the services, he offered a part of his book to his companion, and the twain sang from the same page. The descendants of that woman, if indeed there are any, may well feel pleased to remember, and to talk about the scene in view of the events which have since transpired.

The following incident illustrates the coolness which Mr. Webster exhibited when exposed to danger. When, on one occasion at night, we were returning from Elms Farm in the autumn of 1851, the entire train of cars was thrown off the track, and all broken to pieces, excepting the car in which he was seated. The position into which this car was forced was on the side of a bank, at an angle of forty-five degrees. The moment it was possible, the passengers rushed out in the greatest consternation, and when the writer hurriedly urged him to follow the crowd, he firmly retained his seat, and quietly replied, "Can you inform me to what part of the world we are traveling? I have paid my fare to Boston, and I will thank the locomotive to proceed to its original destination."

And when, a few moments afterward, he saw the locomotive almost in the centre of a neighboring field, and knew that some half dozen cattle had been killed, he repeated his remarks, and threw all who heard him into good humor.

A little incident which occurred only a day or two before Mr. Webster's death, illustrates in some degree the power of a strong will over even an enfeebled frame. A document for the State Department was brought to him to sign. His signature was appended, but by a hand so tremulous that it could hardly be recognized. "Bring me another," said Mr. Webster, cheerfully, as he looked upon his work. "It will never do to send *that* to Washington; they will think it came from a sick man." Then, nerving himself with a strong effort of will, he seized his pen again, and affixed as bold and decided a signature as ever in his days of youthful, healthful prime. "There, that will do," said the expiring secretary, as he sank back again, exhausted.

The gracefulness with which Mr. Webster was in the habit of doing even the most trifling things can hardly be better illustrated than by printing a couple of his autographic notes, of which he must have written many thousands, in reply to earnest solicitations. The following were addressed to the younger daughters of one of his best friends, R. B. Coleman, Esq.:

"Dear Phebe Coleman,

"I was much obliged to your mother for bringing you to see me when I was at the Astor House. I send you my autograph, and pray you to believe that, for your father's and mother's sake, as well as your own, I shall always be your friend,

"Danl. Webster."

"DEAR MISS EMELINE COLEMAN,

"I remember your bright eyes, and am happy to send you an autograph, accompanied with sincere good wishes for your health and happiness.

"DANL. WEBSTER."

These were written from the State Department, and at a moment when he was particularly pressed with the cares of business.

As Mr. Webster has acquired some celebrity as an angler, it may gratify his piscatorial friends to learn when the seeds of this art were planted in his affections. In the spring of his fifth year, when a barefooted boy, he happened to be riding along a road near his birth-place, on the same horse with his father, when the latter suddenly exclaimed, "Dan, how would you like to catch a trout?" Of course, he replied that he would like nothing better; whereupon they dismounted, and the father cut a hazel rod, to which he attached a string and hook out of his pocket, baited it with a worm from under a stone, and told his son to creep upon a rock and carefully throw in on the further side of a deep pool. The boy did as he was bidden, hooked a fish, lost his balance, and tumbled into the water over his head, and was drawn ashore by his father, with a pound trout trailing behind. It has happened to the writer to see the pool in which this trout was captured.

And it may be mentioned as rather a singular fact, that the only law which he drew up and caused to be passed, when for a short time in the Legislature of Massachusetts, was a law for the protection of the common trout and other game fish.

A correspondent furnishes the following anecdote: "It will be recollected that Mr. Webster's continuance in Mr. Tyler's cabinet caused considerable shyness on the part of many of his old political associates toward him. After a brief period, the illustrious statesman concluded the celebrated treaty with England, which won for him a world-wide renown. At this juncture a prominent citizen gave a splendid banquet in Washington, at which were a large number of senators and members of the House of Representatives. The convivialities had just commenced, when the dignified form of Webster was seen entering the parlor, and, as he advanced, his big eyes surveyed the company, recognizing, doubtless, some of those who had become partially alienated from him. On the instant, up sprung a distinguished patriotic senator from one of the large Southern States, who exclaimed, 'Gentlemen, I have a sentiment to propose: The health of our eminent citizen, the negotiator of the Ashburton treaty.' The company enthusiastically responded. Webster instantly replied, 'I have also a sentiment for you: The Senate of the United States, without which the Ashburton treaty would have been nothing, and the negotiator of that treaty less than nothing.' The quickness and fitness of this at once banished every doubtful or unfriendly feeling. The company clustered around the magnate, whose sprightly and edifying conversation never failed to excite admiration, and the remainder of the evening was spent in a manner most agreeable to all."

About the year 1820, Mr. Webster was accustomed to spend the summer months at Dorchester, Massachusetts. Upon his becoming an inhabitant of the town, he called upon the late Dr. Codman, with whom he held similar religious opinions, and remarked, "Sir, I am come to be one of your parishioners—not one of your fashionable ones; but you will find me in my seat both in the morning and in the afternoon." He was true to his word, and a friendship commenced between him and his pastor which continued till the death of the latter, a few years since, and to which Mr. Webster alluded, shortly before his own departure, in terms of affectionate remembrance. Dr. Codman was accustomed to relate the following anecdote of Mr. Webster, which shows, in a singular degree, the wonderful power of fascination which the great orator possessed—the unspoken eloquence, if it may so be termed, of his commanding appearance:

One Sunday afternoon the services of the church were to be conducted by a young student from Andover, who was for the first time to address a large assembly. He commenced reading the opening hymn, but as he proceeded, his voice faltered, and he concluded with difficulty. He sat down, pleading inability to proceed with the other exercises, which the doctor accordingly conducted in his stead.

When questioned, after church, as to the cause of his strange behavior, he replied, that he felt ashamed to acknowledge the truth; but it was, to use his own expression, "those great, black, piercing eyes in the broad aisle that frightened every idea from my head." And he knew not, till he was then told, that Daniel Webster was a member of the congregation.

Among the items of piscatorial information which have dropped from the lips of Mr. Webster are the following: When he was a boy, the imperial salmon, as well as shad, annually visited the Merrimack River in immense numbers; and among the discoveries that he then made was this, that while the latter fish invariably and exclusively ascended the Winnipiseogee, the former never failed to continue their journey further up the Merrimack. It often happened, too, that they left the tide-water in company, but as surely as they approached their parting-place they parted in masses, and were soon as widely removed from each other as honest politicians are from fanatical abolitionists. The discovery in question prompted investigation, when it was found that the temperature of the two streams was very different; for while one of them was rather warm, and ran out of the great Lake Winnipiseogee, the other flowed from the ice-cold springs of the White Mountain; and the further fact was ascertained, that while the shad preferred to cast its spawn in deep and quiet waters, the salmon accomplished the same end in the most shallow and rapid streams among the hills.

Mr. Webster also once mentioned to the writer the following circumstances of a kindred character. In speaking of the blue-fish (the tailor of Chesapeake Bay), he said that its favorite food at the North was the moss-bunker or bony herring, and that it was one of the very few fish which *masticate* their food instead of swallowing it whole; and hence it is that their line of travel is usually designated by an oily scum which covers the water when a school is swimming by. This scum is designated by the fishermen as a *slick*, and when one of them is seen upon the surface of the ocean the fisherman is certain of getting into a school of blue-fish, and of course enjoys fine sport.

In speaking of the tautog or black-fish, he also mentioned the singular circumstance, that it was within his recollection wher this fish was entirely unknown in Massachusetts Bay, though abundant there at the present time. One Captain Crocker transported from Buzzard's Bay to Massachusetts Bay, some fifteen years ago, a large number of these fish, a subscription having been raised by gentlemen of Boston to defray the expenses. This is the origin of the black-fish in Massachusetts Bay. The writer happens to know from experience that it is not taken as far south as Chesapeake Bay, excepting once and a while one in the harbor of Charleston, whose ancestors were transported there a few years ago by way of experiment.

It is also his opinion that the *Maskelonge* was so named by the French, and means *long mask;* and the term pickerel, he thinks, belongs properly to the pike when *half grown.* In speaking of the trout, he was in the habit of calling him the "highway robber of the streams;" and all trout fishers will perceive the appropriateness of the expression.

On one occasion (when first Secretary of State, but at home on a brief visit), he happened to be out fishing for mackerel in his smack, off Marshfield. The fish were abundant, and there was quite a number of local fishermen on the ground. While the sport was at its height, however, Mr. Webster discovered in the offing, rapidly approaching, what he supposed to be a stranger sail. He questioned Seth Peterson in regard to the matter, and was convinced that his *suspicions* and *fears* were correct; whereupon he impatiently demanded in what direction, with the present wind, the smack could sail the fastest? The reply was, "With her eye toward Halifax;" when Mr. Webster exclaimed, "It's a hard case, Skipper, but press forward with all speed, for the master of yonder vessel is evidently an *office-seeker*."

The truth was, there lived a man in the neighboring town of Scituate who had for months past been bothering him for an appointment, so that the fears of the Secretary were well grounded.

Forty years ago a journey from Washington City to New England was an important undertaking, and during the early spring months almost an impossibility. The consequence was, that, at the adjournment of Congress, a party of members from the North would sometimes club together, and, chartering a comfortable vessel, return home by water. Of such a party was Mr. Webster a member in the spring of 1812, and, though they anticipated a tedious voyage, he was the only individual who had the sagacity to take with him a collection of books. Of all those who profited by these books, there was one honorable gentleman who was more famous for his much speaking than for his wisdom, and in this particular not unlike some of his successors of the present day. The first book that he lighted upon was *Gulliver's Travels*, and in this he was so intensely interested as to read it through a number of times, at the expense occasionally of sweet sleep and warm dinners; and when he returned the volume, he thanked Mr. Webster for the use thereof, told him it was one of the most interesting books he had ever read, and then added, "*Do you really believe, sir, that it is an authentic record?*" "As a matter of course," replied Mr. Webster, "since it is distinguished for its remarkable *minuteness*."

Many years ago, when Mr. Webster was traveling through the State of Ohio, accompanied by a friend, he chanced to stumble upon a jovial party of Buckeye farmers who were enjoying the sport of a turkey-shooting match. Having pulled up his horses for the purpose of satisfying his curiosity, he was invited to try his hand, and accepted the offer. He selected what he thought one of the best rifles, examined it with the air of a good shot, raised it to his eye, and sent a bullet directly through the centre of the target. The biggest of the turkeys was immediately presented to him, and then the Buckeye gentlemen worked themselves into a state of excitement as to who the stranger marksman could be. They invited him to partake of a dinner with them at the adjoining tavern, and he assented. While at the table, Mr. Webster's friend thought it his duty to introduce the "great unknown" to the company; and, having done so, what was their astonishment to learn that he was the same man who had delivered a famous speech in Congress. He, of course, gratified his newly-made friends by addressing them a few appropriate remarks; and when he continued his journey, they accompanied him on the way a distance of twenty miles. And they tried hard, too, to induce him to make another of his "crack shots;" but he was, of course, too sagacious to run the risk of losing his recently-acquired reputation.

A writer in the "Virginia Advocate," who happened to hear Mr. Webster's speech in reply to Colonel Hayne, thus uniquely chronicled his opinion of the orator:

"He was a totally different thing from any public speaker I ever heard. I sometimes felt as if I were looking at a mammoth treading, at an equable and stately pace, his native cane-brake; and, without apparent consciousness, crushing obstacles which nature had never designed as impediments to him."

On one occasion, in 1834, just as Mr. Webster had risen in his seat to present a memorial to the Senate, a person seated in the gallery, and having the appearance of a preacher, suddenly shouted out, "My friends, the country is on the brink of destruction. Be sure that you act on correct principles. I warn you to act as your consciences may approve. God is looking down upon you, and if you act upon correct principles you will get safely through." As soon as he had made an end of this brief oration, he very leisurely stepped back, and made his way out of the gallery before the officers of the House had time to reach him. The President and Senate were all surprised, and it was some time before the usual tranquillity was re tored. During the commotion Mr. Webster had remained standing, and the first sentence that he uttered was this: "*As the gentleman in the gallery has concluded, I will proceed with my remarks.*"

When Mr. Webster was at the Capon Springs, the yeomanry of that portion of Virginia came a distance of fifty miles to shake him by the hand, one old Revolutionary soldier having *walked* no less than fifteen miles; and it is said that when he concluded the address there delivered, an old man went toward him with tottering steps, and, having put his arms around him, exclaimed, "God bless you, for you are the greatest and best man in the world!" The address in question had some very eloquent passages, and produced a great sensation.

The following circumstance is a somewhat remarkable instance of the effect of Mr. Webster's eloquence. There had been a constitutional question pending between the Charlestown and Warren bridges, which connect the city of Boston with the main-land, and Mr. Webster had delivered an argument in favor of the former, when the price of the shares thereof immediately rose from two hundred to twelve hundred dollars.

A gentleman of Nantucket once accosted a friend by

saying, "I have wished to see you for some days, for I am in trouble, and wish your friendly advice." "What can it be?" replied the other. "Why, I have a lawsuit, and *Webster* is opposed to me; what shall I do?" "My advice is," was the answer, "that your only chance of escape is to send to Smyrna and *import a young earthquake!*"

When Mr. Webster was in Charleston, South Carolina, in 1847, he concluded a brief speech in the following manner:

"Gentlemen, allow me to tell you of an incident. At Raleigh, a gentleman purposing to call on me, asked his son, a little lad, if he did not wish to go and see Mr. Webster. The boy answered, 'Is it that Mr. Webster who made the spelling-book, and sets me so many hard lessons; if so, I never want to see him as long as I live.'

"Now, gentlemen, I am that Mr. Webster who holds sentiments on some subjects not altogether acceptable, I am sorry to say, to some portions of the South. But I set no lessons. I make no spelling-books. If I spell out some portions of the Constitution of the United States in a manner different from that practiced by others, I readily concede, nevertheless, to all others a right to disclaim my spelling, and adopt an orthography more suitable to their own opinions, leaving all to that general public judgment to which we must, in the end, all submit." And when he took his seat, the following toast was submitted: "Here's to the agreeable schoolmaster—who sets no lessons."

At the time that Colonel Hayne made his attack upon Mr. Webster in the Senate, that paragon of a man and political writer, *Joseph Gales*, *Esq.*, happened to be present. Hearing that Mr. Webster intended to reply, and would probably be quite brief, he resolved to try his hand, for this particular occasion, at his long-neglected vocation of short-hand reporter. He undertook the task, but finding that the "reply" was likely to occupy a number of hours instead of some thirty minutes, the magnitude of the labor that it would be to write out his notes appeared so formidable that he shrunk from it as an impossibility, with the many engagements that demanded his attention. The friends of Mr. Webster urged upon Mr. Gales the imperative necessity of writing out the speech, but the prospect was gloomy, when suddenly an intimation was received from Mrs. Gales (who had in former years been in the habit of assisting her husband in elaborating his reports) that she would do all in her power to write out the speech in full. The result was, that in the course of a week a copy was presented to Mr. Webster in the handwriting of Mrs. Gales, and when published in the *National Intelligencer* had an unprecedented circulation. The original notes, adorned with a few unimportant alterations in the handwriting of Mr. Webster himself, were subsequently neatly bound in a volume, and now constitute one of the attractions of Mr. Gales' private library. And the writer of this paragraph has been informed by Mr. Gales that the superb speech in question was far more brilliant and impressive in its delivery than it now appears upon paper.

In the great argumentative conflict between Mr. Webster and Colonel Hayne, the latter complained of the former's assault upon him instead of Colonel Benton, who had preceded him in the debate, and who was the originator of the controversy. Mr. Webster, who had never thought proper before that time to notice Colonel Benton in debate, replied to Colonel Hayne, "that it was a matter of no consequence who was the drawer, he had found a responsible endorser, and he chose to look to him."

At a dinner party a few evenings thereafter, Mr. Webster and Mr. Preston, of South Carolina (Hayne's successor in the Senate), happened to be placed opposite to each other at table, and were indulging in sportive conversation, when (in reference to something Mr. Webster playfully addressed to a lady beside him) Mr. Preston observed to Mr. Webster, "I will maintain any thing the lady asserts." Mr. Webster replied, "that he should require no endorser for the lady." "And yet," rejoined Mr. Preston, "I have known you to resort to an endorser in preference to a drawer." The allusion was manifest, and though appreciated for its wit, was more highly thought of as evidencing the elevated tone of feeling which could render subservient to purposes of social pleasure even the sharpest weapons of political warfare.

On the evening following the delivery of the reply to Colonel Hayne there was a reception at the White House, and the rival champions happening to be present on the occasion, were of course the lions. The east-room was crowded to excess, and while Mr. Webster stood at one end, chatting with his friends, apparently but little exhausted by the exertion of the day, severe as it had been, the flush of excitement still lingering upon his noble countenance, Colonel Hayne stood at the other, receiving the congratulations of his friends, and bearing himself like a Southern gentleman, as he was in every particular, and as if the idea of being numbered with the vanquished had never entered his mind. With others, he went up to compliment Mr. Webster on his brilliant effort; but, before he had a chance to speak, the former accosted him with his usual courtesy, "How are you this evening, Colonel Hayne?" To which the colonel replied, good-humoredly, "*None the better for you, sir!*"

Portraits and busts of Mr. Webster have been executed almost without number, but no artist has had better opportunities of representing him, or has succeeded more completely than Mr. Healey. His picture of the United States Senate Chamber, as it appeared during the delivery of the famous reply to Colonel Hayne, is a production of merit and value, and a worthy representation of the memorable scene. The subject was, indeed, a passive one, and did not admit of any display of merely physical action, but the interest was that of pure intellect and matter-of-fact patriotism, wherein it differed materially from what are generally termed historical paintings. It is, however, an historical picture of a high order, for it contains veritable portraits of one hundred and thirty persons, a large proportion of whom are distinguished American statesmen; while the remainder are composed of some of the chief literary men of the country, and a few of the ladies who adorned the society of Washington City at the time of the great debate. In the centre of this truly splendid audience stands Mr. Webster, noble beyond compare in mere stature, but with a flood of the most elevated thought beaming from his countenance. He stands directly in front of the President of the Senate (Mr. Calhoun); but instead of looking at him, at his antagonist (Colonel Hayne), or at the audience, he seems to be in a momentary trance, with his eyes fixed on vacancy, as if marshaling his thoughts for this burst of eloquence.

"While the Union lasts, we have high, exciting, gratifying prospects spread out before us, for us and our children. Beyond that I seek not to penetrate the vail. God grant that in my day, at least, that curtain may not rise. God grant that on my vision never may be opened what lies behind. When my eyes shall be turned to behold, for the last time, the sun in heaven, may I not see him shining on the broken and dishonored fragments of a once glorious Union; on states dissevered, discordant, belligerent; on a land rent with civil feuds, or drenched, it may be, in fraternal blood! Let their last feeble and lingering glance rather behold the gorgeous ensign of the Republic, now known and honored throughout the earth, still full high advanced, its arms and trophies streaming in their original lustre, not a stripe erased or polluted, nor a single star obscured; bearing for its motto no such miserable interrogatory as, *What is all this worth?* Nor those other words of delusion and folly, *Liberty first, and Union afterward;* but every where spread all over in characters of living light, blazing on all its ample folds, as they float over the sea and over the land, and in every wind under the whole heavens, that other sentiment dear to every true American heart, LIBERTY AND UNION, NOW AND FOREVER, ONE AND INSEPARABLE!"

Mr. Healey's picture was the result of several laborious years, and he may congratulate himself with the reflection that he has not only produced a work of excellence in itself, both as a gallery of portraits, but as an historical picture, and one also which will increase in value continually.

When he first formed the purpose of painting this picture, he was engaged in executing a series of portraits of the Presidents of the United States, and other distinguished American statesmen, under a commission from the late King of the French, who desired to add them to the great historical collection in the Royal Museum of Versailles. Mr. Healey was also subsequently engaged in painting the portraits of historical personages in England, for the same patron and the same destination, at which time he was kindly permitted to suspend this commission, in order that he might repair to America and paint from life the likenesses introduced in the large picture. Before he could resume his labors in England, the revolution of 1848 terminated the royal commission; but he returned to France with the fruit of his studies and labors in this country, that he might be able to mature the composition and complete the execution of his great picture, with the advantage of constant reference to the productions of the old masters, and in the spring of 1851 the work was completed.

The last daguerreotype portrait of Mr. Webster, taken

in July last, was presented by him to the writer, and, it may be imagined, is treasured with special care; and the only *full-length* daguerreotype of him in existence is the one in the writer's possession. Both of the above were taken at Elms Farm: the latter at the suggestion of the writer, who had asked Mr. Webster to seat himself for only a moment, directly in front of his residence, under a tree that he had planted thirty years ago.

A sanctimonious lady once called upon Mr. Webster, in Washington, with a long and pitiful story about her misfortunes and poverty, and asked him for a donation of money to defray her expenses to her home in a Western city. He listened with all the patience he could manage, expressed his surprise that she should have called upon him for money simply because he was an officer of the government, and that, too, when she was a total stranger to him, reprimanded her in very plain language for her improper conduct, and *handed her a note of fifty dollars.*

The following characteristic anecdote is related of Mr. Webster, and is said to have occurred when he was much engaged in the Senate, at a period of great excitement in the councils of the nation:

He had called upon the cashier of the bank where he kept an account, for the purpose of getting a draft discounted, when that gentleman expressed some surprise, and casually inquired why he wanted so much money? "To spend; to buy bread and meat," replied Mr. Webster, a little annoyed at this speech.

"But," returned the cashier, "you already have upon deposit in the bank no less than three thousand dollars, and I was only wondering why you wanted so much money."

This was indeed the truth, but Mr. Webster had forgotten it. In devoting his mind to the interests of his country, he had forgotten his own.

Those who have blamed Mr. Webster for his occasional apparent indifference to the questions which agitate the public mind will do well to remember that his motto was, that

"*Some questions will improve by keeping.*"

His whole career as a statesman and a diplomatist has illustrated the wisdom of this course of conduct, and, indeed, it is the only one upon which a solid and permanent reputation can be built. The history and present position of the journal known as the *National Intelligencer* constitute another prominent illustration of the truth of the motto.

It is undoubtedly a fact beyond dispute, that no American has been more frequently entertained at complimentary dinners, during the last half century, than Mr. Webster; and it has occurred to the writer that his readers might be pleased to peruse the following toasts or sentiments. They are selected from a large number of similar character, and may be considered as fairly echoing the opinions of the public in regard to their distinguished subject:

Bangor.

Daniel Webster. The pride of his country and the glory of human nature.

Hallowell.

Our distinguished Guest. The Granite State has the honor of his birth, the Bay State of his residence, but to the Federal Union belong his services and talents.

The Granite State. She has well deserved the name, since she has produced a mighty rock, our only defense against general corruption.

Boston.

Our distinguished Guest. Worthy the noblest homage which freemen can give or a freeman receive—the homage of their hearts.

Concord.

Daniel Webster. A working-man of the first order. New Hampshire rejoiced in the *promise* of the *youth;* his country now glories in the *performance* of the *man.*

New York.

Our Guest, Daniel Webster. To his talents we owe a most triumphant vindication of the great principles of the Constitution.

The State of Massachusetts. Honored in a citizen who is received with the acclamations of the world.

Albany.

The Constitution of the United States and Daniel Webster, inseparable now, and inseparable in the records of time and eternity.

Syracuse.

The Constitution and its greatest expounder; the Union and its ablest defender.

Baltimore.

Daniel Webster. His countrymen award him the proudest honors of statesmanship, and the republic has recorded his services on the enduring pillars of her Union.

His country will never forget that his fame has extended her own among the nations of the world.

Capon Springs.

Daniel Webster, our distinguished Guest. The jurist and statesman, who has illustrated the glory of our country. The champion of the Constitution and the Union, who has sown the seed of constitutional liberty broadcast over the world.

Annapolis.

Daniel Webster. Maryland shows her attachment to the Union by honoring its ablest defender.

Cincinnati.

The Constitution of the United States. Ambiguous and obscure only to the ambitious and corrupt; when assailed by such, may there ever be found among the people a DANIEL *who can interpret the writing.* He may be cast among *lions*, as many as you please; but even there will he be found the master-spirit.

The following was sent to a dinner-party by a lady:

Daniel Webster.

"Westward the Eastern star has bent its way,
May *more* than empire bless its cloudless ray."

Charleston.

Our Guest. He has a heart big enough to comprehend his whole country—a head wise enough to discern her best interests; we cheer him on his way to view her in all her various aspects; well assured that the more he sees of her the better he will like her.

And it may be well to mention here that the town of Salem, Massachusetts, claims the honor of having been the first to toast him as the *Defender of the Constitution.* The exact reading of the toast, as the Hon. Edward Everett informed the writer, was as follows: "The highest honors of the Constitution to its ablest defender."

Letters of inquiry have frequently been written to Mr. Webster respecting the authenticity of the famous speech introduced by him as that of John Adams's, in his discourse on the death of Adams and Jefferson, at Faneuil Hall, in 1826, and the following is one of his replies. The speech in question was simply an effort, founded upon a custom of the ancient historians.

"Washington, December 31st, 1849.

"Dear Sir,

"I have had very frequent occasions to answer the same inquiry as that which you propose to me in your letter of the 26th of this month. The speech to which you refer is my composition. The Congress of the Revolution sat with closed doors, and there is no report of the speeches of members on adopting the Declaration of Independence. We only know that John Adams spoke in favor of the measure with his usual power and fervor. In a letter, written from Philadelphia soon after the Declaration was made, he said it was an event which would be celebrated in time to come by bonfires, illuminations, and other modes of public rejoicing. And on the day of his death, hearing the ringing of bells, he asked the occasion, and being told that it was the 4th of July, and that the bells were ringing for Independence, he exclaimed, 'Independence forever!" These expressions were used, in composing the speech, as being characteristic of the man, his sentiments, and his manner of speech and elocution. All the rest is mine.

"With respect, your obedient servant,

"Danl. Webster.

"Samuel N. Sweet, Esq."

In another letter upon the same subject, he writes, "The speech was written by me, in my house in Boston, the day before the delivery of the discourse in Faneuil Hall. A poor substitute, I am sure, it would appear to be, if we could now see the speech actually made by Mr. Adams on that transcendently important occasion."

Mary Russell Mitford, in her recently published "Recollections of a Literary Life," gives us the following particulars:

"One of the greatest, if not the very greatest, of the living orators of America, is, beyond all doubt, Daniel Webster. That he is also celebrated as a statesman and a lawyer, is a matter of course in that practical country, where even so high a gift as eloquence is brought to bear on the fortunes of individuals and the prosperity of the commonwealth; no idle pilaster placed for ornament, but a solid column aiding to support the building. A column, indeed, stately and graceful, with its Corinthian capital, gives no bad idea of Mr. Webster; of his tall and muscular person, his massive features, noble head, and the general expression of placid strength by which he is distinguished. This is a mere fanciful comparison; but Sir Augustus Callcott's fine figure of Columbus has been reckoned very like him—a resemblance that must have been fortuitous, since the picture was painted before the artist had ever seen the celebrated orator. When in England some ten or twelve years ago, Mr. Webster's calm manner of speaking excited much admiration, and perhaps a little surprise, as contrasted with the astounding and somewhat rough rapidity of progress which is the chief characteristic of his native land. And yet that calmness of manner was just what might be expected from a countryman of Washington; earnest, thoughtful, weighty, wise. No visitor to London ever left behind him pleasanter recollections, and I hope that the good impression was reciprocal. Every body was delighted with his geniality and taste; and he could hardly fail to like the people who so heartily liked him. Among our cities and our scenery, he admired that most which was most worthy of his admiration; preferring, in common with many of the most gifted of his countrymen, our beautiful Oxford, whose winding streets exhibit such a condensation of picturesque architecture, mixed with water, trees, and gardens, with ancient costume, with eager youth. with by-gone associations and rising hope, certainly to any of our new commercial towns, and perhaps, as mere picture, to London herself; and carrying home with him, as one of the most precious and characteristic memorials of the land of his forefathers, a large collection of architectural engravings, representing our magnificent Gothic cathedrals, and such of our Norman castles and Tudor manor-houses as have escaped the barbarities of modern improvers. We are returning ourselves to that style now; but twelve years ago it was his own good taste, and not the fashion of the day, that prompted the preference. I owe to his kindness, and to that of my admirable friend, Mr. Kenyon, who accompanied him, the honor and pleasure of a visit from Mr. Webster and his amiable family in their transit from Oxford to Windsor. My local position between these two points of attraction has often procured me the gratification of seeing my American friends when making that journey. But during *this* visit a little circumstance occurred, so characteristic, so graceful, and so gracious, that I can not resist the temptation of relating it.

"Walking in my cottage garden, we talked naturally of the roses and pinks that surrounded us, and of the different indigenous flowers of our island and of the United States. I had myself had the satisfaction of sending to my friend, Mr. Theodore Sedgwick, a hamper containing roots of many English plants familiar to our poetry; the common ivy—how could they want ivy who had had no time for ruins?—the primrose, and the cowslip, immortalized by Shakspeare and by Milton; and the sweet-scented violets, both white and purple, of our hedgerows and our lanes; that known as the violet in America (Mr. Bryant somewhere speaks of it as 'the yellow violet') being, I suspect, the little wild pansy (viola tricolor), renowned as the love-in-idleness of Shakspeare's famous compliment to Queen Elizabeth. Of these we spoke; and I expressed an interest in two flowers known to me only by the vivid description of Miss Martineau: the scarlet lily of New York and of the Canadian woods, and the fringed gentian of Niagara. I observed that our illustrious guest made some remark to one of the ladies of the party; but I little expected that, as soon after his return as seeds of these plants could be procured, I should receive a package of each, signed and directed by his own hand. How much pleasure these little kindnesses give! And how many such have come to me from over the same wide ocean!"

As Coleridge said of Southey, Mr. Webster "possessed, but was not possessed by, his genius." No man ever had his powers more completely under command. At a moment's warning the vast stores of his mind were ready, and the most impromptu speech rolled from his tongue in perfect composition. He was always logical in conversation—this was his great characteristic—enchained the attention of every listener by the driest argument, and had a manner of the most singularly mixed grace and power. His eloquence, when he warmed, was perfectly overpowering, and then he came out with a flow of poetry which would hardly be thought possible from the severe cast of his mind. Harriet Martineau, who met him at a dinner-party at the British legation at Washington, said there was no merrier man. She describes him as leaning back at his ease on the sofa, shaking it with burst after burst of laughter, telling stories, cracking jokes, or smoothly discoursing to the perfect felicity of the logical part of one's constitution. Such was his private boon companionship. Abroad, however, he was the stern, plain-dressed, grave republican; and the common man who passed him in the street thought he could read the cares and responsibilities of the whole United States government on his great brow.

"As a lawyer, pursuing his professional avocations in the judicial courts," wrote the same lady, in her "Society in America," "and as a member of the Senate, he has ever formed a striking character. In the Supreme Court, where he has often plead before the judges, and in which many of those masterly forensic arguments were delivered that constitute a considerable portion of his published productions, he is described by an eye-witness as sometimes standing firm as a rock, while listening to the chief justice delivering a judgment; his large, cavernous eyes wide awake, his lips compressed, and his whole countenance in that intent stillness which instantly fixes the eyes of the stranger. It was not uncommon for him to saunter into the court, throw himself down, and lean back against the table, while seeming to see nothing about him; and there was no knowing whether he would by-and-by go away, or whether he would rouse himself suddenly and stand up to address the judges. Still, however it might turn out, it was amusing to see how the court would fill after the entrance of Mr. Webster, and empty when he had returned to the Senate Chamber. In his pleading, as in his speaking in the Senate, it was interesting to see one so dreamy and *nonchalant* roused into strange excitement. It was something to watch him moved with anxiety in the toil of intellectual conflict; to see his lips tremble, his nostrils expand, the perspiration start upon his brow; to hear his voice vary with emotion, and to trace the expression of laborious thought, while he paused for minutes together, to consider his notes and decide upon the arrangement of his argument.

"In the Senate his services have always been acknowledged to be invaluable; he there displayed industry, energy, and sound-headedness. He spoke but seldom; but when he did so, it was generally on some constitutional question, where his logical powers and legal knowledge were brought into play, and where his authority was considered oracular by assemblages of the first men in the country. When speaking to the Senate, he invariably manifested great earnestness, and seemed to believe every sentiment he uttered; and he convinced by appealing to the reasoning powers of his listeners rather than to their passions. Before entering on the delivery of a speech, on one occasion, he might be seen, absent and thoughtful, making notes. When he rose, his voice was moderate and his manner quiet, with the slightest possible mixture of embarrassment, his right hand resting upon his desk, and the left hanging by his side. Before his first head was finished, however, his voice would rise so as to fill the chamber, and ring again to the remotest corner; then he would fall back into his favorite attitude, with his left hand under his coat skirt and his right in full action. At this moment the eye would rest upon him as upon one inspired, seeing the invisible and grasping the impalpable. When the vision had passed away, the change was astonishing; he sat at his desk writing letters or dreaming, so that he did not always discover when the Senate was going into a division. Some one of his party had not seldom to jog his elbow, and tell him that his vote was wanted."

The most complete edition of Mr. Webster's writings which has yet appeared was published in the spring of this year (1852), by Little & Brown, Boston. It was edited by the Hon. Edward Everett, and made six large handsome volumes. To each of these is prefixed a Dedication by Mr. Webster, and their exceeding beauty is the writer's apology for reprinting them in this place. They also show that he was warm-hearted.

FIRST VOLUME.

To my Nieces,

MRS. ALICE BRIDGE WHIPPLE,

and

MRS. MARY ANN SANBORN.

"Many of the speeches contained in this volume were delivered and printed in the lifetime of your father, whose fraternal affection led him to speak of them with approbation.

"His death, which happened when he had only just passed the middle period of life, left you without a father, and me without a brother.

"I dedicate this volume to you, not only for the love I have for yourselves, but also as a tribute of affection to his memory, and from a desire that the name of my brother,

"EZEKIEL WEBSTER,

may be associated with mine, so long as any thing written or spoken by me shall be regarded or read.

"DANL. WEBSTER."

SECOND VOLUME.

To

ISAAC P. DAVIS, ESQ.

"MY DEAR SIR,

"A warm private friendship has subsisted between us for half our lives, interrupted by no untoward occurrence, and never for a moment cooling into indifference. Of this friendship, the source of so much happiness to me, I wish to leave, if not an enduring memorial, at least an affectionate and grateful acknowledgment.

"I subscribe this volume of my speeches to you.

"DANL. WEBSTER."

THIRD VOLUME.

To

CAROLINE LE ROY WEBSTER.

"MY DEARLY BELOVED WIFE,

"I can not allow these volumes to go to the press without containing a tribute of my affection, and some acknowledgment of the deep interest that you have felt in the productions which they contain. You have witnessed the origin of most of them, not with less concern, certainly, than has been felt by their author; and the degree of favor with which they are received by the public will be as earnestly regarded, I am sure, by you as by myself.

"The opportunity seems, also, a fit one for expressing the high and warm regard which I ever entertained for your honored father, now deceased, and the respect and esteem which I cherish toward the members of that amiable and excellent family to which you belong.

"DANL. WEBSTER."

FOURTH VOLUME.

To

FLETCHER WEBSTER, ESQ.

"MY DEAR SON,

"I dedicate one volume of these speeches to the memory of your deceased brother and sister, and I am devoutly thankful that I am able to inscribe another to you, my only surviving child, and the object of my affections and hopes. You have been of an age, at the appearance of most of these speeches and writings, at which you were able to read and understand them; and in the preparation of some of them you have taken no unimportant part. Among the diplomatic papers there are several written by yourself, wholly or mainly, at the time when official and confidential connections subsisted between us in the Department of State.

"The principles and opinions expressed in these productions are such as I believe to be essential to the preservation of the Union, the maintenance of the Constitution, and the advancement of the country to still higher stages of prosperity and renown. These objects have constituted my pole-star during the whole of my political life, which has now extended through more than half the period of the existence of the government. And I know, my dear son, that neither parental authority nor parental example is necessary to induce you, in whatever capacity, public or private, you may be called to act, to devote yourself to the accomplishment of the same ends.

"Your affectionate father,

"DANL. WEBSTER."

"My dear Sir,

"The friendship which has subsisted so long between us springs not more from our close family connection than from similarity of opinions and sentiments.

"I count it among the advantages and pleasures of my life; and I pray you to allow me, as a slight but grateful token of my estimate of it, to dedicate to you this volume of my speeches. Danl. Webster."

SIXTH VOLUME.

"With the warmest paternal affection, mingled with deeply afflicted feelings, I dedicate this, the last volume of my works, to the memory of my deceased children

"JULIA WEBSTER APPLETON,

beloved in all the relations of daughter, wife, mother, sister, and friend; and

"MAJOR EDWARD WEBSTER,

who died in Mexico, in the military service of the United States, with unblemished honor and reputation, and who entered that service solely from a desire to be useful to his country and do honor to the state in which he was born.

"'Go, gentle spirits, to your destined rest:
While I, reversed our nature's kindlier doom,
Pour forth a father's sorrow on your tomb.'

"Danl. Webster."

As the devoted affection which existed between Daniel Webster and his brother Ezekiel was one of the peculiarities of their lives, and as they also resembled each other in many particulars, both physical and intellectual, it can not but be proper to insert in this place a brief sketch of the latter gentleman, from the pen of the late Samuel L. Knapp.

"Ezekiel Webster was two or three years older than his brother Daniel, but did not graduate until three years after him, in 1804. In college he was the first in his class; his intellect was of a very high order; its capacity was general, for he was able to comprehend the abstruse and difficult, and at the same time to enjoy the tasteful and the elegant. He was distinguished for classical literature; his knowledge of Greek, particularly, was beyond that of his contemporaries in college; his knowledge of English literature was deep and extensive, for he had not skimmed over books as a matter of amusement, but he looked into them as a man of mind, who intends to draw lessons from all he reads. Few men among our scholars knew so much of the English poets as he did; and he valued them as he should have done, as philosophers and painters of human nature, from whom much knowledge may be obtained to illustrate and adorn what duller minds have put into maxims and rules.

"He made himself master of the law as a science, and became well acquainted with its practice in his native state. He went up to first principles with the ease and directness of a great mind, and separated at once that which was casual and local from that which is permanent, and founded on the basis of moral justice and the nature of man. There seemed no effort in any thing he did;

all was natural and easy, as if intuitive. There was nothing about him of that little bustling smartness so often seen in ordinary persons striving to perform something to attract the attention of the little world around them.

"His general information was not only extensive, but laid up in excellent order, ready for use. He was steadily engaged in the duties of his profession, but never seemed hurried or confused in his business; he took all calmly and quietly; he did nothing for parade or show, or mere effect, nor did he speak to the audience while addressing the court and jury. His life was passed in habits of industry and perseverance, and his accumulations of wealth and knowledge were regular and rapid. From the commencement of his life, as a reasonable being responsible for his own actions, to the close of it, he preserved the most perfect consistency of character; no paroxysms of passion, no eccentricities of genius, were ever found in him. His equanimity was only equaled by his firmness of purpose. In this he was most conspicuous; he thought leisurely and cautiously, and having made up his mind, he was steadfast and immovable. Having no hasty or premature thoughts, he seldom had occasion to change his opinions, and was therefore free from those mortifying repentances so common to superior minds of warmer temperament. By honesty of purpose and soundness of judgment he kept a just balance in weighing all matters before him. All his firmness and equanimity, and other virtues, seemed constitutional, and not made up by those exertions so necessary to most frail beings who intend to support a character for steady habits. He was blessed with a frame that felt few or no infirmities. He suffered no moral or mental weakness in his whole path of duty, for his constitution, until within a short time of his death, exhibited a sound mind in a sound body, and neither appeared essentially injured or decayed to the hour of his exit from the world.

"He never sought public honors, nor literary or political distinctions, and therefore had none of those throes and agonies so common to vaulting ambition; not that he declined all public trusts, when he was conscious that he could do any good to his fellow-men. He was several years a member of one or other branch of the Legislature of New Hampshire, and served as a trustee of Dartmouth College. He was at different times put up for a member of Congress; but it was at periods when his friends thought that his name would do some good to his political party, as the members of Congress in New Hampshire are chosen by a general ticket; but when they were decidedly in power, he would seldom or never consent to be a candidate. This was much to be regretted, for he was admirably calculated for public life by his extensive knowledge and incorruptible integrity. He would have been a first-rate speaker on the floor of Congress. His eloquence was impressive and commanding. There was in his delivery a slight defect in the labial sounds, in the familiar use of his voice, which was rather pleasant to the listener than otherwise, for it was a proof of a natural manner; but, warmed by his subject, a more rich, full, and sonorous voice was seldom heard in any public body; not that his tones were delicate or mellifluous, but full of majesty and command; free from arrogance, timidity, or hesitation. His gestures were graceful, but not in the slightest degree studied; his language was rich, gentlemanly, select, but not painfully chosen; he not only had words for all occasions, but the very words he should have used.

"As a writer, he excelled in judgment and taste; there was a classical elegance in his familiar writings; and his higher compositions were marked with that lucid order, and clearness of thought, and purity of expression, which distinguished the Augustan Age. His sentences were not grappled together by hooks of steel, but connected by golden hinges that made a harmonious whole. His library was rich in works of merit, ancient and modern. The history of literature and science was as familiar to him as that of his native state, and he had the means of turning to it with much greater facility. He was an instance in point that a man may be a good lawyer, and yet devote some of his time to classical pursuits.

"Ezekiel Webster was one of those great men, rare instances in the world, who had thrown away ambition, and who professed to be learned and happy in his course of life, rather than to court the gale and spread his sails to be wafted along on popular opinion. He sought not popularity, but he had it; *that popularity which follows, not that which is run after.* He watched the signs of the times, and was as good a diviner in politics as any one; but, whatever the presages were, he looked at coming events unmoved, leaving their results to Heaven.

"For several of the last years of his life, he was curtailing his business in order to devote some portion of the prime of his manhood to literary and scientific pursuits, so congenial to his heart; but in this he was disappointed, for, while yet in the fullness of his strength, he was called to leave the world, for whose benefit he was formed. His death was sudden and remarkable; he fell and expired while in the midst of an argument at the bar, without a sigh or a struggle. No event could have been more unexpected by the public, for he was one of those models for a picture of health and strength that Salvator Rosa would have drawn in his mountain scenery, if he had wished to exhibit a commander able to bear the fatigues and duties of council and of war. He was lamented by his professional brethren, and sincerely mourned by the community at large."

H

ILLNESS AND DEATH.

WEEP not, weep not for the mighty dead! In the sunset of his days, and the plenitude of his fame, Daniel Webster has passed from among the living. His great spirit ascended to the skies through the peaceful atmosphere of a Sabbath morning, and while the glory of Autumn was upon the land. And this was well; for, through life, he habitually hallowed the Sabbath, and loved, above all others, the closing season of the year. But what is more, he died a Christian. With all his intellect, when he came to resign his soul into the keeping of his Creator, he did it with a prayer for mercy, and with the meekness and confidence of a little child. Who, then, can for an instant doubt that he is now in heaven? As surely as there is an All-merciful Savior, he must be among the redeemed. He lived as this nation would have its subjects live, and died the pride of nature, and, beyond all question, the well-beloved child of God.

He occupied, more completely than any other man of his age, the "*vantage-ground*" to do his country good, and therefore he deserves the fame of having been an "*honest man.*" If honest, he was true; and if true, he was true to his God, to his country, to his fellow-men, to his family, and true to himself. And thus he died, one of the best of men, and the foremost intellect of his time.

But, alas! it is also true, to use the eloquent figure of a chief mourner, the "heart of the nation throbs heavily at the portal of Webster's tomb." There are private griefs, however, wholly to the world unknown. Among those who knew him well and sincerely loved him, I claim the right and the privilege to be numbered. On the lonely sea, whose ground-swell was an emblem of his beating heart—among his native mountains, and in the sanctuary of his sick-chamber, have I been his sole companion. He was to me like a father, and he uttered words to me which I hold sacred as my life. My own feelings toward him were those of unbounded admiration; and yet, when enjoying his companionship alone, our relative positions seemed mutually to be forgotten; he descended to my level, and I only thought of loving him, and doing my all to make him happy. And now, as I think upon his pleasant ways, his kindly smiles and words, and his noble deeds, I feel as if my pen, from very weakness, should abandon its present task. Let, then, the voice of eulogy be uttered every where by the gifted and the good who have studied his intellectual character, while I content myself by recording some of the more interesting facts attending his decline and death.

I date his more rapid decline from the autumn of last year, at which time he was afflicted with one of the severest attacks of his annual catarrh. I was with him during its entire continuance, and I remember well that I wondered how any man could endure so much bodily suffering without a murmur. This singular cold or disease was one which had come upon him at a particular period of the year—late in August—for upward of twenty years, with the single exception of the summer that he visited England. From the autumn of 1851 until the hour of his death, he was, to my mind, upon the inclined plane of death. I believed this from what I saw, and the belief was confirmed by what he sometimes uttered. He often alluded to himself as an old man, and, when in certain moods, loved to talk about the quiet home appointed for all living. I most firmly believe what I now utter, and I utter the opinion out of justice to the dead and charity for the living. He had too powerful a mind to be killed by disappointment, and though it may be well to let the motto pass as a poetic and just punishment, it is not true that, as a cause and a consequence, he was "*rejected and lost.*" The word President would only have dimmed the lustre of the name of Daniel Webster; and if we must sorrow that what men expected can never come to pass, let us not weep for him, but for his country.

And his physicians tell us that his decline was hastened by the accident which befell him in the spring of the present year. Surely I have cause to feel a terrible interest in this conclusion. I was with him at the time, seated by his side in his own carriage, and I held the reins. It was about nine o'clock in the morning, and we were on our way to Plymouth on a pleasure excursion. It was while he was talking about the hardships endured by the Pilgrim fathers, and while our eyes rested upon the memorable bay, that, in the twinkling of an eye, we were both thrown from the carriage on account of the breaking of the transom bolt. Not a bit of harm was done to my own worthless body, and, on recovering from the shock, I hastened to his rescue. When I lifted him up, and saw blood clotted with dust streaming down his dome-like forehead, I felt as if the very sky would fall and crush me to the earth. I helped him, however, into a neighboring house, kind friends placed him in a bed, and a physician was soon in attendance. He was quite faint for a time, and as he lay in this state, the interest manifested by those who had come in to see him was intense. Among those who stood by was a gentleman, over eighty years of age, who had long been a personal friend of his. This person was watching the wounded man with most painful anxiety; but when Mr. Webster, in answer to some question put to him by the doctor, replied with promptness, the old man suddenly exclaimed, "*Thank God, he has his reason!*" and, bursting into tears, wept like a child. I subsequently mentioned this fact to Mr. Webster, and he said that he had noticed the whole of it himself, and was affected by the recollection. After remaining near the scene of the accident (which was twelve miles from home, and only one from Plymouth) about four hours, he was conveyed to Marshfield, and there remained confined to his bed and room for about ten days. At that time he was not known to have been injured internally, but both his arms were very severely bruised and sprained, so that he could not write his name for many weeks. During the few days immediately succeeding the accident, he was perfectly helpless, and suffered very great pain, and yet he was cheerful, and told an unusual number of anecdotes. During this period it was that he sent me to the library for a copy of Milton, and bade me read the first canto aloud "slowly and distinctly." As I did so, he would occasionally interrupt me for the purpose of descanting upon certain ideas that he thought "*wonderfully grand and beautiful.*" While yet his arms were confined in a sling, though in other respects quite well, he amused himself by walking about the mansion—now peering into a closet or trunk filled with musty papers, which had been hidden from his sight for many years, and now suggesting all sorts of little improvements for the comfort and convenience of the household. And twenty times in the day, when the mood was upon him, would he visit the extensive apartments where were congregated his overseer, the various assistants, and his servants, and for every one he had a playful compliment and the kindest words. He had a fashion of designating me as the "*colonel*," and on one occasion during this period, he said that he intended to make a "general" of me, if I would only continue, until he was well again, to *open the doors, or force a way at his command.* In themselves, these little incidents are mere trifles, but their association with the greatest mind of this country renders them interesting, and I trust the reader will forgive my egotism.

It is somewhat singular that Mr. Webster's two last speeches were delivered while upon a kind of triumphal march—one of them in Boston, and the other at Marshfield; and it is also strange but providential, that he should finally have been permitted to die at home and surrounded with his kindred. The reception which he met with in the former place was the most splendid demonstration of the kind ever witnessed in the country. I never saw a more interesting spectacle than was presented in front of the Revere House, when he returned to his lodgings at the twilight hour in a carriage completely filled with flowers, drawn by six white horses, and escorted by a cavalcade of nearly one thousand horsemen in military array. The speech which he delivered to an immense multitude on that occasion was worthy of his fame, and yet, in his own opinion and in the opinion of his friends, he was at that time a sick man.

But the moral grandeur of his reception at Marshfield, now that his body is in the tomb, positively seems almost sublime. He came, as it were, from a field of intellectual conquest, where he had battled forty years for his country—a conquest such as the world had seldom or perhaps never before witnessed. A procession, consisting of thousands of his neighbors, without respect to party, met him at a point eight miles distant from his residence, and escorted him home, while the road was literally lined with women and children to welcome him, and garlands without number were strewn along his pathway. Upon a hill, in the immediate vicinity of his mansion, the great concourse came to a halt; they delegated an orator to welcome him with a speech, and his reply was beautiful and appropriate to the many, but to the few who lived in his shadow there was a tone of sadness in all he uttered. He finished his address just as the sun was setting, and I can not but think of it as one of the golden clouds which will be remembered with the glory of his own departure into the night of death. It was the last he ever uttered to a public assembly. And now I remember how, after the crowd had disappeared, he entered his mansion fatigued beyond all measure and covered with dust, and threw himself into a chair. For a moment his head fell upon his breast, as if completely overcome, and he then looked up like one seeking something which he could not find. It was the portrait of his darling but departed daughter Julia, and it happened to be in full view. He gazed upon it for some time in a kind of trance, and then wept like one whose heart was broken, and these words escaped his lips: "*Oh, I am so thankful to be here! If I could only have my will, never, never would I again leave this home!*" And then he sought and obtained a night of repose. He made one more visit to the seat of government, wound up to all intents and purposes his affairs, and now his manly form is in that sleep which knows no waking.

The last time that he ever attended church, it was my rare fortune to be his companion. He had been informed that the Rev. E. N. Kirk, of Boston, was expected to preach in Duxbury, some three miles from Marshfield, and packing off his guests and a part of his household in a couple of carriages, he reserved a gig for himself, and in this did we attend. The sermon was on the efficacy of prayer, and was distinguished not only for its eloquence, but for its powerful arguments. It dealt in nothing but pure Bible doctrines as understood by the orthodox Church. Mr. Webster listened with marked attention to the whole discourse, and, after the services were closed, went up and congratulated the preacher. On our return home, his conversation turned upon the sermon, and he said it was a remarkable, a great effort. He said the arguments adduced were unanswerable, and that if a man would only live according to the lessons of such preaching, he would be a happy man both in this world and the world to come. He said, moreover, "There is not a single sentiment in that discourse with which I do not fully concur." And this remark, when appended, as it ought to be, to the sermon when hereafter published, will serve to convince the world that his views of religion were most substantial and satisfactory. During the whole of our ride home, he conversed upon matters contained in, or suggested by the discourse, and I deeply regret that I did not take more ample notes of what he said on the occasion. The distinct impression left upon my mind, however, was that if he were not a genuine Christian, the promises of the Bible were all a fable; and God knows that I would rather die than, for a moment, even imagine such a state of things.

He was a believer in the Great Atonement; and though, living as he did in a sphere of peculiar temptations, he may have committed errors, he needed no promptings to lead him to a speedy repentance. He was actuated by a spirit of charity which knew no bounds. He treasured no animosities to his fellow-men, and when once wronged by those in whom he had confided with all the guilelessness of a child, he did not retaliate, but simply moved in another sphere beyond their reach. He was a student of the Bible, and read it habitually in his family whenever the annoyances of his official position did not prevent; and never sat down, when with his family alone, to enjoy the bounties of his table, without first imploring a blessing.

No man ever thought or talked with more reverence of the power and holiness of God. He came of a race of good men; was baptized into, and became a member, in his college days, of the Congregational Church, but died in the communion of the Protestant Episcopal Church, of which he was a devout member; and one of the most impressive scenes that I ever witnessed, going to prove the matchless beauty of our religion, was to see him, in full view of the Capitol, the principal theatre of his exploits, upon his knees before the altar partaking of the sacrament of the Lord's Supper. That spectacle, and the grandeur of his death, are to me more eloquent than a thousand sermons from human lips.

In his personal appearance Mr. Webster was an extraordinary man, and at the age of forty was considered the handsomest man in Congress. He was above the ordinary size, and stoutly formed, but with small hands and feet, had a large head, very high forehead, a dark complexion, large black, deeply-sunken, and solemn-looking eyes, black hair (originally), very heavy eyebrows, and fine teeth. To strangers his countenance appeared stern, but when lighted up by conversation, it was bland and agreeable. He was slow and stately in his movements, and his dress was invariably neat and elegant; his favorite suit for many years having been a blue or brown coat, a buff vest, and black pantaloons. His manner of speaking, both in conversation and debate, was slow and methodical, and his voice generally low and musical, but when excited, it rang like a clarion.

The more rapid decline of Mr. Webster commenced while

at Marshfield, about one week before his death, which occurred just before three o'clock on Sunday morning, the twenty-fourth of October. He was in the seventy-first year of his age, and had, therefore, just passed the allotted period of human life. He looked upon his coming fate with composure and entire resignation. On the afternoon of the twenty-third, he conversed freely, and with great clearness and detail, in relation to the disposal of his affairs. His last autograph letter was addressed to the President; and among the directions that he gave respecting his monument was, that it should be no larger than those erected to the mother of his children, and to Julia and Edward. He dictated an epitaph, which will in due time be published.

At five o'clock he was seized with a violent nausea, and raised considerable dark matter tinged with blood, which left him in a state of great exhaustion and debility. The physician in attendance, Dr. John Jeffries, then announced to Mrs. Webster that his last hour was rapidly approaching. He received the announcement calmly, and directed all the females of the family to be called into the room, and addressed to each of them individually a few affectionate parting words, and bade them a final farewell. He then took leave of his male relatives and personal friends, including his farmers and servants, addressing each individually in reference to their past relations, and bade each an affectionate adieu. The last of his family that he parted with was Peter Harvey Webster, a grandson, the child of Fletcher Webster, for whom he invoked the richest blessings of Heaven. He then said, as if speaking to himself,

"On the twenty-fourth of October all that is mortal of Daniel Webster will be no more." In a full and clear voice he then prayed most fervently, and impressively concluded as follows: "Heavenly Father, forgive my sins, and welcome me to thyself, through Christ Jesus." Dr. Jeffries then conversed with him, and told him that medical skill could do nothing more, to which he replied, "Then I am to be here patiently till the end: if it be so, may it come soon." His last words were, "*I still live;*" and, coming from such lips, it seems to me they can not but fully convince the most hardened skeptic of the immortality of the soul. They seem to fall upon the ear from beyond the tomb, and to be the language of a disembodied spirit passing into paradise. During his last hour he was entirely calm, and breathed his life away so peacefully that it was difficult to fix the precise moment that he expired.

He died, according to Dr. Jeffries, of disease of the liver. The immediate cause of his death was hemorrhage from the stomach and bowels, owing to a morbid state of the blood consequent upon the above disease. There was also dropsy on the abdomen. On making a post-mortem examination, it was found that the cerebral organs were of the very largest known capacity, exceeding, by thirty per centum, the average weight of the human brain; and with only two exceptions (Cuvier and Dupuytren), the largest of which there is any record. It is also worthy of remark, that a well-marked effusion upon the arachnoid membrane was discovered, although there were no perceptible evidences of any lesion during Mr. Webster's lifetime. It is supposed to have been caused by his severe fall from his carriage in Kingston last spring. It is a remarkable physiological fact, that an injury that would have impaired the intellect, if not at once caused death in another, should in this instance have been attended with so little external evidence of so important an injury to a vital organ.

He left a will, which was dictated and signed on the third day preceding his death, the contents of which I do not think it proper to mention at this time. His literary executors were Edward Everett, George Ticknor, George T. Curtis, and C. C. Felton, who will in due time present the country with a rich store of literary wealth. He did not forget his friends, but left to many of them slight memorials of his attachment.

His remains were embalmed, and, instead of a shroud, were arrayed in a suit like that he was sometimes fond of wearing in other days—a blue coat with gilt buttons, white cravat, vest, pantaloons, and gloves, silken hose, and shoes of patent leather. His coffin, with only his name upon it, was elegant but unpretending; and while it remained under the roof of the Marshfield mansion, stood upon his own favorite writing-table, in the centre of the library, the spot of all others which he loved for the sake of his darling child Julia, who had designed it for him; and the spot, too, with which are associated some of the most happy, and altogether the most salutary recollections of my life. He was the best friend I ever had, and as he taught me all I know, God grant that I may hereafter emulate his manifold virtues.

The day of his funeral, the twenty-ninth of October, was

sunny and cheerful, and his remains were escorted to the tomb by some ten thousand friends, countrymen, and lovers, among whom were many of the most illustrious men of the country. The services were performed by the Rev. *Ebenezer Alden*, the pastor of the orthodox Congregational Church of the town, and were as simple and unpretending as had been the inner life of the departed. And when the pall of night settled upon the earth, the long rank grass upon the tomb of Daniel Webster mingled its rustling with the sighing of the breeze, and the low, mournful requiem of the ocean.

CONCLUDING NOTE.

While this work was going through the press, a request was made of the author that he should reserve, for the more legitimate use of Mr. Webster's literary executors, a certain collection of private letters which he was known to have in his possession. The propriety of the request was so apparent, it was, of course, willingly complied with, and it is to be hoped that the official presentation to the public of all Mr. Webster's correspondence and other literary remains will not be long delayed. The letters herein published have already appeared in the public journals, and were, of course, common property, and, as such, were simply employed to illustrate the unvarnished records of fact and affection.

APPENDIX.

APPENDIX.

EULOGY IN BOSTON.

THE following masterly effort of requiem-eloquence was delivered at a public meeting of the citizens of Boston, by the Hon. Edward Everett. This gentleman was a devoted friend and companion of the departed for a much longer period than any other man now living, and this fact alone is deemed a sufficient apology for giving it a place in this volume, in preference to the equally brilliant efforts of a hundred others, who have given expression to their great admiration and their deep sorrow. It is copied from the report as published in the newspapers.

"MR. MAYOR AND FELLOW-CITIZENS,

"I never rose to address an assembly when I was so little fit, body or mind, to perform the duty; and I never felt so keenly how inadequate are words to express such an emotion as manifestly pervades this meeting in common with the whole country. There is but one voice that ever fell upon my ear which could do justice to such an occasion. That voice, alas! we shall hear no more forever. No more at the bar will it unfold the deepest mysteries of the law; no more will it speak conviction to admiring

Senates; no more in this hall, the chosen theatre of his intellectual dominion, will it lift the soul as with the swell of the pealing organ, or stir the blood with the tones of a clarion in the inmost chambers of the heart.

"We are assembled, fellow-citizens, to pour out the fullness of our feelings; not in the vain attempt to do honor to the great man who is taken from us; most assuredly, not with the presumptuous hope, on my part, to magnify his name and his praise. They are spread throughout the land. From East to West, and from North to South (which he knew, as he told you, only that he might embrace them in the arms of loving patriotism), a voice of lamentation has already gone forth, such as has not echoed through the land since the death of him who was first in war, first in peace, and first in the hearts of his countrymen.

"You have listened, fellow-citizens, to the resolutions which have been submitted to you by Colonel Heard. I thank him for offering them. It does honor to his heart, and to those with whom he acts in politics, and whom I have no doubt he well represents, that he has stepped forward so liberally on this occasion. The resolutions are emphatic, sir, but I feel that they do not say too much. No one will think that they overstate the magnitude of our loss, who is capable of appreciating a character like that of Daniel Webster's. Who of us, fellow-citizens, that has known him—that has witnessed the masterly skill with which he would pour the full effulgence of his mind on some contested legal and constitutional principle, till what seemed hard and obscure became as plain as day;

who that has seen him, in all the glory of intellectual ascendency—

"'Ride on the whirlwind and direct the storm'

of parliamentary conflict; who that has drunk of the pure fresh air of wisdom and thought in the volumes of his writings; who, alas! sir, that has seen him

"'———— in his happier hour
Of social pleasure, ill exchanged for power,'

that has come within the benignant fascination of his smile, has felt the pressure of his hand, and tasted the sweets of his fireside eloquence, will think that the resolutions say too much?

"No, fellow-citizens, we come together not to do honor to him, but to do justice to ourselves. We obey an impulse from within. Such a feeling can not be pent up in solitude. We must meet, neighbor with neighbor, citizen with citizen, man with man, to sympathize with each other. If we did not, mute nature would rebuke us. The granite hills of New Hampshire, within whose shadow he drew his first breath, would cry shame; Plymouth Rock, which all but moved at his approach; the slumbering echoes of this hall, which rung so grandly with his voice; that 'silent but majestic orator,' which rose in no mean degree at his command on Bunker Hill—all, all would cry out at our degeneracy and ingratitude.

"Mr. Chairman, I do not stand here to pronounce the eulogy of Mr. Webster; it is not necessary. Eulogy has already performed her first offices to his memory. As the mournful tidings have flashed through the country, the highest offices of nation and state, the most dignified official bodies, the most prominent individuals, without distinction of party, the press of the country, the great voice of the land, all have spoken, and with one accord of opinion and feeling; and a unanimity that does honor at once to the object of this touching attestation, and to those who make it. The record of his life, from the humble roof beneath which he was born, with no inheritance but poverty and an honored name, up through the arduous paths of manhood, which he trod with lion heart and giant step, till they conducted him to the helm of state—this stirring narrative, not unfamiliar before, has, with melancholy promptitude, within the last three days, been again sent abroad through the length and breadth of the land. It has spread from the Atlantic to the Mississippi. Struggling poverty has been cheered afresh; honest ambition has been kindled; patriotic resolve has been invigorated; while all have mourned.

"The poor boy at the village school has taken comfort as he has read that the time was when Daniel Webster, whose father told him that he should go to college if he had to sell every acre of his farm to pay the expense, laid his head on the shoulder of that fond and discerning parent, and wept the thanks he could not speak. The pale student, who ekes out his scanty support by extra toil, has gathered comfort when reminded that the first jurist, statesman, and orator of the time earned with his weary fingers, by the midnight lamp, the means of securing the same advantages of education to a beloved brother. Every true-hearted citizen throughout the Union has felt an honest pride, as he reperuses the narrative, in reflecting that he lives beneath a Constitution and a government under which such a man has been formed and trained, and that he himself is compatriot with him. He does more, sir; he reflects with gratitude that, in consequence of what that man has done, and written, and said—in the result of his efforts to strengthen the pillars of the Union—a safer inheritance of civil liberty, a stronger assurance that these blessings will endure, will descend to his children.

"I know, Mr. Mayor, how presumptuous it would be to dwell on any personal causes of grief, in the presence of this august sorrow which spreads its dark wings over this land. You will not, however, be offended if, by way of apology for putting myself forward on this occasion, I say that my relations with Mr. Webster run further back than those of almost any one in this community. They began the first year he came to live in Boston. When I was but ten or eleven years old, I attended a little private school in Short Street (as it was then called; it is now the continuation of Kingston Street), kept by the late Hon. Ezekiel Webster, the elder brother to whom I have alluded, and a brother worthy of his kindred. Owing to illness, or some other cause of absence on his part, the school was kept for a short time by Daniel Webster, then a student of law in Mr. Gore's office; and on this occasion, forty-seven or forty-eight years ago, and I a child of ten, our acquaintance, since then never interrupted, began.

"When I entered public life, it was with his encouragement. In 1838, I acted, fellow-citizens, as your organ in the great ovation which you gave him in this hall. When he came to the Department of State in 1841, it was on his recommendation that I, living in the utmost privacy beyond the Alps, was appointed to a very high office abroad; and in the course of the last year, he gave me the highest proof of his confidence, in intrusting to me the care of conducting his works through the press. May I venture, sir, to add, that in the last letter but one which I had the happiness to receive from him, alluding, with a kind of sad presentiment which I could not then fully appreciate, but which now unmans me, to these kindly relations of half a century, he adds, 'We now and then see, stretching across the heavens, a clear, blue, cerulean sky, without cloud, or mist, or haze. And such appears to me our acquaintance from the time when I heard you for a week recite your lessons in the little school-house in Short Street, to the date hereof,' twenty-first July, 1852.

"Mr. Chairman, I do not dwell upon the traits of Mr. Webster's public character, however tempting the theme. Its bright developments in a long life of service are before the world; they are wrought into the annals of the country. Whoever in after times shall write the history of the United States for the last forty years, will write the life of Daniel Webster; and whoever writes the life of Daniel Webster as it ought to be written, will write the history of the Union from the time he took a leading part in its concerns. I prefer to allude to those private traits which show the MAN, the kindness of his heart, the generosity of his spirit, his freedom from all the bitterness of party, the unaffected gentleness of his nature. In preparing the new edition of his works, he thought proper to leave almost every thing to my discretion, as far as matters of taste are concerned. One thing only he enjoined upon me with an earnestness approaching to a command. 'My friend,' said he, 'I wish to perpetuate no feuds. I have lived a life of strenuous political warfare. I have sometimes, though rarely, and that in self-defense, been led to speak of others with severity. I beg you, where you can do it without wholly changing the character of the speech, and thus doing essential injustice to me, to obliterate every trace of personality of this kind. I should prefer not to leave a work that would give unnecessary pain to any honest man, however opposed to me.'

"But I need not tell you, fellow-citizens, that there is no one of our distinguished public men whose speeches contain less occasion for such an injunction. Mr. Webster habitually abstained from the use of the poisoned weapons of personal invective or party odium. No one could more studiously abstain from all attempts to make a political opponent personally hateful. If the character of our congressional discussions has of late years somewhat declined in dignity, no portion of the blame lies at his door. With Mr. Calhoun, who for a considerable portion of the time was his chief antagonist, and with whom he was brought into most direct collision, he maintained friendly relations. He did full justice to his talents and character. You remember the feelings with which he spoke of him at the time of his decease. Mr. Calhoun, in his turn, entertained a just estimate of his great opponent's worth. He said toward the close of his life, that of all the leading men of the day, 'there was not one whose political course had been more strongly marked by a strict regard to truth and honor than Mr. Webster's.'

"One of the resolutions speaks of a permanent memorial to Mr. Webster. I do not know what is contemplated, but I trust that such a memorial there will be. I trust that marble and brass, in the hands of the most skillful artists our country has produced, will be put in requisition to reproduce to us—and nowhere so appropriately as in this hall—the lineaments of that noble form and beaming countenance on which we have so often gazed with delight. But after all, fellow-citizens, the noblest monument must be found in his works. There he will live and speak to us and our children when brass and marble have crumbled into dust. As a repository of political truth and practical wisdom applied to the affairs of government, I know not where we shall find their equal. The works of Burke naturally suggest themselves to the mind as the only writings in our language that can sustain the comparison. Certainly no composition in the English tongue can take precedence of those of Burke in depth of thought, reach of forecast, or magnificence of style. I think, however, it may be said, without partiality, either national or personal, that while the reader is cloyed at last with the gorgeous finish of Burke's diction, there is a severe simplicity and a significant plainness in Mr. Webster's writing that never tires. It is precisely this which characterizes the statesman in distinction from the political philosopher. In political disquisition elaborated in the closet, the palm must, perhaps, be awarded to Burke over all others, ancient or modern. But in the actual conflicts of the Senate, man against man, and opinion against opinion; in the noble war of debate, where measures are to be sustained and opposed, on which the welfare of the country and the peace of the world depend; when often the line of intellectual battle is changed in a moment; no time to reflect, no leisure to cull words or gather up illustrations, but all to be decided by a vote, although the reputation of a life may be at stake; all this is a very different matter, and here Mr. Webster was immeasurably the superior. Accordingly, we find, historically (incredible as it sounds, and what I am ready to say I will not believe, though it is unqestionably true), that these inimitable orations of Burke, which one can not read without a thrill of admiration to his fingers' ends, actually emptied the benches of Parliament. Ah! gentlemen, it was very different with our great parliamentary orator. He not only chained to their seats willing, or, if there was such a thing, unwilling senators, but the largest hall was too small for his audience. On the memorable 7th of March, 1850, when he was expected to speak upon the great questions then pending before the country, not only was the Senate Chamber thronged to its utmost capacity at an early hour, but all the passages to it, the rotunda of the Capitol, and even the avenues of the city, were alive with the crowds who were desirous of gaining admittance. Another senator, not a political friend, was entitled to the floor. With equal good taste and good feeling, he stated that 'he was aware that the great multitude had not come together to hear him; and he was pleased to yield the floor to the only man, as he believed, who could draw together such an assembly.' This sentiment, the effusion of parliamentary courtesy, will, perhaps, be found no inadequate expression of what will finally be the judgment of posterity.

"Among the many memorable words which fell from the lips of our friend just before they were closed forever, the most remarkable are those which my friend Hilliard has just quoted: 'I STILL LIVE!' They attest the serene composure of his mind, the Christian heroism with which he was able to turn his consciousness in upon itself, and explore, step by step, the dark passage (dark to us, but to him clearly lighted from above) which connects this world with the world to come. But I know not, Mr. Chairman, what words could have been better chosen to express his relation to the world he was leaving: 'I still live! This poor dust is just returning to the dust from which it was taken; but I feel that I live in the affections of the people to whose service I have consecrated my days. I still live! The icy hand of Death is already laid on my heart, but I still live in those words of counsel which I have uttered to my fellow-citizens, and which I now leave them as the last bequest of a dying friend.'

"Mr. Chairman, in the long and honored career of our lamented friend, there are efforts and triumphs which will hereafter fill one of the brightest pages in our history. But I greatly err if the closing scene—the height of the religious sublime—does not, in the judgment of other days, far transcend in interest the brightest exploits of public life. Within that darkened chamber at Marshfield was witnessed a scene of which we shall not readily find the parallel. The serenity with which he stood in the presence of the King of Terrors, without trepidation or flutter, for hours and days of expectation; the thoughtfulness for the public business, when the sands were so nearly run out; the hospitable care for the reception of the friends who came to Marshfield; that affectionate and solemn leave separately taken, name by name, of wife, and children, and kindred, and friends, and family, down to the humblest members of the household; the designation of the coming day, then near at hand, when 'all that was mortal of Daniel Webster would cease to exist!' the dimly recollected strains of the funeral poetry of Gray, last faint flash of the soaring intellect; the feebly murmured words of the Holy Writ repeated from the lips of the good physician, who, when all the resources of human art had been exhausted, had a drop of spiritual balm for the parting soul; the clasped hands; the dying prayers: oh! my fellow-citizens, this is a consummation over which tears of pious sympathy will be shed ages after the glories of the forum and the Senate are forgotten.

"'His sufferings ended with the night,
Yet lived he at its close;
And wore the long, long night away
In statue-like repose.
Yet ere the sun in all its state
Illumed the eastern skies,
He passed through glory's morning gate,
And walked in Paradise!'"

EULOGY IN NEW YORK.

The following brief eulogy was delivered by Hiram Ketchum, Esq., in New York, and is here published for the same reasons that were offered in regard to Mr. Everett's. It was addressed to the bar of the city:

"The offices of this day belong less to grief and sorrow than congratulation and joy. It is true that our illustrious countryman, Daniel Webster, is no longer numbered among the living; but it is a subject of congratulation that he lived beyond the ordinary period allotted to human life, and that he was permitted to die as he had lived, for thirty years in the service of his country; and at his own home, in his own bed, surrounded by his domestic family and friends. The great luminary of the bar, the Senate, and the Council Chamber is set forever, but it is a subject of rejoicing that it is set in almost supernatural splendor, obscured by no cloud; not a ray darkened.

"I have often heard Mr. Webster express a great dread, I may say horrible dread, of a failure of intellect. He did not live long enough to experience such failure. I rejoice that he lived long enough to collect, and supervise, and publish to the world his own works. Many of our distinguished countrymen live only in tradition; but Daniel Webster has made up the record for himself; a record which discloses, clear as light, his political, moral, and religious principles—a record containing 'no word which, dying, he might wish to blot,' or any friend of his desire to efface. More than any living man, he has instructed the whole generation of American citizens in their political duties, and taught the young men of the country how to think clearly, reason fairly, and clothe thought in the most simple and beautiful English. He has reared his own monument. 'There it stands, and there it will stand forever!' The rock which was first pressed by the feet of the Pilgrims first landing on the shores of this Western Continent is destined long to be remembered; but not longer than the oration commemorating that event, delivered two hundred years after it occurred, by Daniel Webster.

"The monument which indicates the spot where the first great battle of the American Revolution was fought will stand as long as monumental granite can stand; but long after it is obliterated and scattered, the oration delivered on laying its corner-stone, and the other oration, pronounced nineteen years after, on its completion, will live to tell that such a monument was. The names of John Adams and Thomas Jefferson will be known to a distant futurity; but I believe that among the last records which will tell of their names will be the eulogy, of which they were the theme, pronounced by Daniel Webster. We all hope, and some of us believe, that the Constitution and Union of our country will be perpetual; but we know that the speeches and orations in defense and commendation of that Constitution and Union delivered by Daniel Webster will live as long as the English language is spoken among men. I might refer to the Capitol of the country, to every important institution, and every great name in our land among the living and the dead, for there is not one of them that has not been embalmed in his eloquence

"In the few remaining remarks which I have to make," continued Mr. Ketchum, "allow me, sir, to speak of some of the personal characteristics of Mr. Webster as they have fallen under my own observation. I have long been acquainted with him. From all I know, have seen and heard, I am here to-day to bear testimony that Daniel Webster, as a public man, possessed the highest integrity. He always seemed to me to act under the present conviction that whatever he did would be known not only to his contemporaries, but to posterity. He was 'clear in office.' He regarded political power as power in trust; and though always willing and desirous to oblige his friends, yet he would never, directly or indirectly, violate that trust. I have known him in private and domestic life. During the last twenty-five years I have received many letters from him; some of which I yet retain, and some have been destroyed at his request. I have had the pleasure of meeting him often in private circles and at the festive board, where some of our sessions were not short; but neither in his letters nor his conversation have I ever known him to express an impure thought, an immoral sentiment, or use profane language. Neither in writing nor in conversation have I ever known him to assail any man. No man, in my hearing, was ever slandered or spoken ill of by Daniel Webster. Never in my life have I known a man whose conversation was uniformly so unexceptionable in tone and edifying in character. No man ever had more tenderness of feeling than Daniel Webster. He had his enemies as malignant as any man; but there was not one of them who, if he came to him in distress, would not obtain all the relief in his power to bestow. To say that he had no weaknesses and failings would be to say that he was not human. Those failings have been published to the world, and his friends would have no reason to complain of that if they had not been exaggerated. It is due to truth and sound morality to say, in this place, that no public services, no eminent talent, can or should sanctify errors. It was one of Mr. Webster's characteristics that he abhorred all affectation. That affectation, often seen in young men, of speaking in public upon the impulse of the moment, without previous thought and preparation, of all others he most despised. He never spoke without previous thought and laborious preparation. As was truly said by my venerable friend who just sat down (Mr. Staples), he was industrious to the end. When, on leaving college, he assumed the place of teacher in an academy, in an interior town of New England, the most intelligent predicted his future eminence. After his first speech in court, in his native state, a learned judge remarked, 'I have just heard a speech from a young man who will hereafter become the first man in the country.' The predictions that were made of Daniel Webster's career were not merely that he would be a great man, but the *first man.*

"I have often thought that if other men could have been as diligent and assiduous as Mr. Webster, they might have equaled him in achievement. When he addressed the court, the bar, the Senate, or the people, he ever thought he had no right to speak without previous preparation. He came before the body to which he was to speak with his thoughts arrayed in their best dress. He thought this was due to men who would stand and hear him, and the result was that every thing he said was always worthy of being read; and no public man in our country has ever been so much read.

"It may be conceded (whether it was a virtue or a weakness) that Daniel Webster was ambitious. He was. He desired to attain high position, and to surpass every man who had occupied the same before him. He spared no labor or assiduity to accomplish this end. Whether he has succeeded or not, posterity must say. I will add, that it is true that he desired the highest political position in the country; that he thought he had fairly earned a claim to that position. And I solemnly believe that because that claim was denied, his days were shortened. I came here, sir, to speak of facts as they are; neither to censure or to applaud any man or set of men; whether what has been done has been well done, or what has been omitted has been well omitted, the public must decide. May I be permitted to add that, though I am no man's worshiper, I have deeply sympathized in thought, in word, and in act with that desire of Mr. Webster? I have continued this sympathy with that desire to the last moment of his life. If there be honor in this, let it attach to me and mine; if disgrace, let it be visited upon me and my children."

THE END.

www.ingramcontent.com/pod-product-compliance
Lightning Source LLC
LaVergne TN
LVHW011208110826
845150LV00006B/1366
* 9 7 8 1 4 2 5 5 1 8 6 1 5 *